MUSLIMS IN INDIA

MUSLIMS IN INDIA

RECENT CONTRIBUTIONS TO LITERATURE

ON

RELIGION, PHILOSOPHY, HISTORY & SOCIAL ASPECTS

DR. MOHAMED TAHER
M.A (Hist.)
M.A (Isl. St.)
M. Lib. Sc.
Ph. D. (Lib. Sc.)
Deputy Librarian
American Studies Research Centre
Hyderabad - 500007.

Introduction by:
Mrs. Rafat Durdana Jalaluddin
M.A (Eng.)
M. Phil (Eng.)
P.G.D.T.E.

ANMOL PUBLICATIONS PVT LTD
New Delhi-110 002

ANMOL PUBLICATIONS PVT LTD
4374/4B, Ansari Road, Daryaganj
New Delhi-110 002

Muslims in India

ISBN 81-7041-620-5
Reprint 1996

PRINTED IN INDIA
Published by J.L. Kumar for Anmol Publications Pvt Ltd, New Delhi-110 002 and Printed at Mehra Offset Press, Delhi.

DEDICATED TO
my wife

Ameena bint Abdur Rasheed Sait

PREFACE

This handy bibliography is a result of painful searches of literature on Muslims in India. It lists all books published anywhere in the world. In limiting to only books (than all forms of published/unpublished sources) it serves as a Books-in-print—i.e., availability of titles in market. Most books are usually identified when these are no more in the market, or become out-of-print. This compilation serves the concerned users with recency of information.

The bibliography presents a holistic approach to the study of the second large majority of the subcontinent. While there are a few attempts to compile bibliographies on this subject, there is none which is comprehensive, upto-date, exhaustive and representative of global contributions. The ones which exists are listed in the chapter on Information sources. This chapter is a bibliography of bibliographies, and also includes bibliographies and bibliographic essays in periodicals.

SCOPE OF THE BIBLIOGRAPHY

It is limited to English language books and bibliographic sources which have appeared from 1970 to 1989. Books published in India on the subject and published elsewhere form the contents of this unique and original work. By subject, its scope is both inter- and multi-disciplinary. A glance at the contents page would support this trans-disciplinary coverage. Being first part of the project, this bibliography, covers in a humble way, all recent books. The second part of the proposed project would be retrospective in nature. The arrangement of the bibliographic sources is based on a scheme, in a modified format, as given in *Islam: Outline of a Classification Scheme* (London, Bingley, 1979).

CONTENTS

INTRODUCTION

THE ADVENT OF ISLAM IN INDIA

1.1 MUSLIM PERIOD

The presence of Muslims in Western and South-Western India can be traced from the time of the second Caliph of Islam, Umar Bin Khattab (634-644). The Arab invasion of Sind took place in 711 and the relationship of the Muslim Arabs with India was "more or less a passing phase."[1] The Arab rulers of Sind established military camps in cities and left the civil administration in the hands of the local rulers; they did not deprive the masses of the privileges which they enjoyed in the earlier reigns. They only asked for the people's submission to them and the payment of the Jaziya or maintenance tax. They remained aloof from the social life of the people and the country. It was in the eleventh century that almost the whole of Western Pakistan and parts of Indian Punjab were annexed to the Ghazni empire by Mahmud of Ghazni who attacked India several times between 1000 and 1026 A.D. The Ghaznaides ruled over the Punjab for about two centuries. Lahore became the eastern-most centre of Persian culture. The Perso-Turks decided to make India their home. Turko-Persian administrative institutions were introduced into India, which later became the basis of the administrative set up of the Delhi Sultanate and still later in some degree of the Mughal Empire. It was only then that "a new culture, a new way of life, a new religion, a new view of art and architecture was grafted into this country."[2] Since then the Perso-Turks, the Mughuls and others professing Islam, who founded dynasties in different parts of the country, had made India their home land. They became the sons of the soil like the Dravidians and the Aryans of remote past. With the initiation of Islam into the

Indian life this country was confronted with a new process of cultural development.

In the last quarter of the 12th century there arose another power from the rugged mountains in Afghanistan, that is, Muhammad Ghori, who established himself at Ghazni driving the last of the Ghaznaides to Lahore in 1178 A.D. Between 1175 and 1186 A.D., he annexed the Muslim Kingdoms of what is now West Pakistan, and conquered almost the whole of northern India and established the Delhi Sultanate.

The establishment of the Delhi Sultanate marked the beginning of the Muslim history in India. With the passage of time the administrative network expanded and colonisation was peaceful. By the fourteenth century the Muslim ruling class acquired a cosmopolitan character. Though there were frequent dynastic changes at the capital, the Delhi Sultanate provided a stable organization of government and powerful judiciary. It protected its subjects from lawlessness and the people could follow their pursuits in comparative security. It reopened and maintained trade-routes and gave a new impetus to internal and external trade leading to the growth of the country's economy.

The hundred and fifty years preceding the establishment of the Mughul Empire under Akbar, constitute a period of turmoil in the Indian Muslim history. The Central authority under the later Tughlaks, the Sayyeds, the Lodhis, the Afghans and the early Mughals was unable to check the birth and growth of such kingdoms. Independent princes sprang up in Kashmir, Bengal, Kandesh, Rajputana, Orissa and the Deccan. Though dynastic in character the new kingdoms symbolized, to some extent, the growing regional loyalties in various parts of India. Regional languages, music, architecture, painting and other forms of art began to develop and acquire regional characteristics. It as in this period that definitive cultural patterns began to evolve in various regions. But, before these cultural regions could fully develop and cultural identity could lead to political identity, they were absorbed by the mighty Mughul empire of Akbar and his successors.

Medieval India, particularly the Mughul period, was very rich in terms of culture. The Muslim contribution in the fields of architecture, painting, music, literature and sculpture was immense. It enriched Indian culture by freely borrowing from the Persian, Central Asian and Chinese.

Thus by the end of the sixteenth century, after a long process of conquest and consolidation, a composite, harmonious, politically strong, economically sound and culturally rich society came into existence. The Mughuls ruled India and enriched its culture and economy. They treated their subjects with tolerance and established harmonious relationships between the Muslim and non-Muslim subjects. They had trade relations with the French, the Dutch and the English. During the Mughul rule the English came to India as tradesmen. They organized themselves into the East India Company, a British trading establishment, which gradually turned from a trading company into a military power with designs to acquire political supremacy. The inefficient later Mughuls, with their weak administration and internal feuds gave the British an opportunity to interfere with the administration of provinces and the settling of disputes between them. The Mughuls had already begun losing power to the Marathas, the Jats, the Sikhs and finally they lost it to the more powerful British.

By 1766 the English East India Company had conquered most of the eastern part of the empire; with the assistance of the East India Company the Qudh ruler defeated the Rohillas. In 1782 the Marathas conquered Delhi and the entire Mughul empire was dismembered.

The British gradually strengthened their hold on the political situation. There was a rapid expansion of British dominion in India during the period 1757-1818. The thorough establishment of the British rule in India affected the different classes of Muslims differently, and the nature of the response of the Muslims to the British rule assumed different forms. We shall attempt to analyse, in the following section, the response to and relationship of the muslims with the British Government and how the Muslim Community emerged as a formidable force in Indian life during the period 1818-1947.

1.2 BRITISH PERIOD

The rapid expansion of British dominion in India during the period 1757-1818 brought a great change in Indian life. The Muslims found it extremely difficult to reconcile with the facts. They could not forget the fact that they had just lost their seven hundred years of rule over the subcontinent, and therefore, could not accept the British supremacy at any cost. This made it extremely difficult for the Muslims to make a satisfactory adjustment with the British rule. For the Hindus there was no such psychological difficulty. They found it not at all difficult to accept the Western authority. They easily took up English in place of Persian and "participated in trade, industry, and banking along with their British principals."[3] The implications of the supersession of the old medieval Muslim empire by the new Western imperial authority were first experienced by the Muslim feudal Lords and artisans in Bengal because Bengal was the headquarters of the East India Company. In medieval north India, the Muslim ruling class had enjoyed special privileges and immense economic power flowing from feudal ownership of vast tracts of land. In 1793, the East India Company carried out the Permanent Revenue Settlement of Cornwallis in Bengal and gave a server blow to Muslim aristocracy there. At the same time the flow of textile from Manchester to India ruined the Bengali artisanship and handloom industry. And on the religious plane, the introduction of the Common Penal Code and separate judicial courts greatly reduced the religious and social authority of the Muslim religious scholars — the Ulama.

The religious, leaders of Delhi were not blind to what was happening in Bengal. To emancipate the Muslims from this bondage and degradation several Muslim Ulama launched socio-religious reform movements in the beginning of the 19th century, more precisely called the Faraizi and the Wahabi movements.[4]

These movements were mainly religious in character and were directed towards purifying Islam in India by removing un-Islamic traits and influences from it. In the agrarian sphere these movements stood for defending the socio-economic interests of the peasants against the Zamindars and the European indigo-planters. In the religious sphere these movements strengthened the processes of Islamisation of the community. Pan-Islamic ideas were infused into the body-politic of the Muslims by the Faraizis-Wahabis. In a political sense these movements were directed against the British rule. The leaders of these movements resented the downfall of the Muslim political power and after long thinking they came to understand that the only hope of arousing the Muslims for re-establishing their rule in India lay in a parallel movements for pure Islam.

These movements did certainly help to remove the depression into which the Muslims had fallen, particularly in the political and economic spheres. Being politically defeated the Muslim leaders sought to reform the community through religious revitalisation in order to attain an overall revolution. But they could not explain to the Muslim masses the problems of their political defeat in terms of concrete political realities. They could not explain to the community for what political and economic reasons the British were successful in establishing their dominion in India. For this reason the history of these movements makes it plain that they registered only reactions not remedies, to the situation then existing."[5]

These religious reform movements which acquired an anti-British character lost their tempo by the end of the 19th century. They inadvertently hightened the British hostility towards the Muslims. And the hostility was only strengthened by the nation wide war of 1857. Some British officers held the view that the 'Sepoy mutiny' as they called it, was initiated and inspired by the Muslims. Henry Thomas of the Bengal Civil Service, writing in 1858 about the revolt remarks that "it was the result of a Mohammadan conspiracy. Left to their resources, the Hindus never would or could have compassed such an undertaking ..." (*Modern Islam in India*, 1946). The British were under this impression probably because the person Installed back as an emperor after the revolt of 1857 was Bahadurshah Zafar, a Muslim. Otherwise, historically speaking it was a joint effort of the entire Indian community, irrespective of religious beliefs.

1.2.1 Social and Cultural Conditions of the Muslims

When one takes an objective view of the nearly ten centuries of the Muslim presence in India — at a glance — one gathers that they were disproportionately dispersed over the whole of the country, spoke the language of the provinces they inhabited and participated generously in the social, political, economic and cultural life of the provincial social groups of which they formed an integral part. Prior to the arrival of the British the relationship of the Muslims with other religious groups was very cordial and warm. There were hardly any instances of clashes on the basis of religion and community. They constituted the ruling class at a point of time in history in certain parts of the country and in certain other parts (as under the Sikhs and the Marathas) they were the ruled community. As rulers they were, generally liberal, broad-minded and large-hearted, as ruled they were sincere and cooperative.

Community consciousness, religious bigotry and feelings of antagonism between the Muslims and the Hindus of India began with the arrival of British. The British government made it a policy of its administration to divide the two communities and secure its own ends. When it found it difficult to implement measures against the common stand of Indian people, it sought to divide them and make them class conscious and group conscious so that their opinion got divided and their loyalties got submerged. Thus the British made it a policy of its administration to divide and rule throughout its reign.

When the Indian Muslims understood the British policy they felt infuriated but had to suppress their fury. Many a time they tried to bring unity in their Hindu breathern in order to give a blow to the British policy. They felt the British were their enemy rather than their benefactors. They saw in the British rule an alien rule which barred their normal social, economic and cultural development and which could not see them united. This kind of national sentiment arose among the Indians because the British rule imposed certain basic handicaps on the free development of the nation which was their (the Britisher's) subject. The revolt of 1857 revealed for the first time that a large scale alliance between the Hindus and the Muslims against the British was possible and would be fruitful.

There is no doubt that the Muslims found it psychologically difficult to tear themselves away from their past. But the treatment meted out by the British made it even more difficult for them to adjust themselves with the present. Though they had ceased to be the governing class in India, they looked upon their past with pride. They still considered themselves as the aristocratic class of the country. "This complex among the Muslims deterred them from taking to anything British (English education for instance) in large numbers."[6] Eventually it alienated them from the British, and created difference between them and the Hindus for the latter took to British education and culture very easily.

As a result there was a marked discrimination in the British treatment of the Muslims. When the Muslims were loyal to the British policies they gained in grants, if they were indifferent they suffered confiscation. As the Punjabi Muslims were loyal to the British they gained in grants of land and in so far as the Bengali Muslims were aloof, they continued to suffer exclusions from official employment.[7]

In Bengal the position of Muslims was exactly the opposite of that of Uttar Pradesh. Here they were backward both economically and educationally. The peramanent settlement of Cornwallis had elevated the Hindu collectors to the position of landlords and had given them the opportunity to amass wealth which would otherwise have fallen to the share of the Muslims. Besides the fear that deterred Muslims from taking to English education there, is another factor responsible for their educational backwardness. The lower class Muslims did not have enough opportunities to benefit from English education. About 85% of Muslims in North Bengal were agriculturalists and it was not within their means to afford English education. In the provinces where they were engaged in trade and commerce, as in Bombay and U.P., they did show keenness to go for it.[8] Gradually the Indian Muslim society experienced a qualitative structural transformation during the British rule which led it on a new and different path of development. The British rule initiated some of the basic changes in social physiognomy though to subserve its own interests. "It generated new currents in the economic processes, though as a colony of British capitalism. It inaugurated new principles of political structure, established different criteria of sovereignty and devised different norms of governance. It generated forces which directly and indirectly gave mortal blows to the Indian cultural and religious values."[9] "The British Rule inaugurated a qualitative structural transformation which hitched the Indian Muslim society to a new path (of modernism).[10] Once the forces of modernism started working there was no strong force to check them. In spite of organized attempts by religious movements to stem the tide of modernism, the results were shortlived. The endeavour made by various classes and strata to meet the challenge of the situation created by the British manifested itself in movements which created a new exciting, interesting, heroic and unique history for the Indian people. The reactions and movements being basically against the British rule manifested themselves into an all-India Muslim awakening.

1.2.2 Social Movements and Organisations

After the British took over the Indian administration dethroning the ineffective Mughul ruler, the Indian Muslim community arrived at a turning point. Due largely to the discriminatory treatment of the British, and also due to their own inability to face the social and political reality with courage, the Muslims gradually developed the attitude of a defeated community with a negative outlook. As the community entered the 20th century it appeared to be in a hopeless position. Politically beaten, economically backward, intellectually moribund and religiously medieval, there seemed to be no adequate base for contending with the modern forces it would encounter. Its particular concern in those day was only to preserve its cultural heritage which was its only unassailable possession. Creative thinking, and experimental approach to life had no place in its scheme of things, even moderate progress was far from being achieved. In all respects the Muslims seemed ill-prepared to face the multifarious challenges approaching them.

Time and its pressures, however, altered the situation. The pressures issuing from the changing social context included: the challenge for socio-political competition from other communities — particularly the Hindus; the problem of unemployment; the growth of western-style education against the religious one. These pressures touched hard the Muslim viewpoint; as a result social and political leadership had to gradually compel them to emerge out of the dark.

1.2.2.1 Two Influential Schools of Thought: Deoband and Aligarh

There were basically two schools of thought that led the Muslims into action in the 19th Century, out of an atmosphere of inaction. These were the Deoband School of thought and the Aligarh School of thought. There is a marked difference between the two. Though both the schools worked for the survival and uplift of the Muslims — one was religious, with pan-Islamic ideas and anti-British objectives and the other was secular and pro-British.

The Deoband school was based on the Walliullahi tradition which was a pan-Islamic anti-British tradition.[11] The main aim of the several workers of the Deoband school was to "re-establish contact between the Muslim Ulama and the average Muslim masses, and to reorientate the Muslim community to its original cultural and religious identity.[12] With the Deoband Seminary as its centre, the Ulama of this school of thought—Moulana Qasim Nanawtvi, Moulana Mahmud Hasan and Maulana Abdul Bari of farangi Mahal — made efforts "to spread, through education, among the religious class of Muslims, the spirit of freedom."[13] All its leaders were staunch enemies of the British. They did not tolerate anything British — neither dress, food, language, customs nor traditions. But they remained aloof from politics excepts for issuing a fatwa to the Muslims to support the Indian National Congress. As the school remained indifferent to practical politics, which stems from its aversion of the British, its fervour for political freedom devoid of political action, did not take any concrete political organizational shape.[14] Keeping to the values of religious fundamentalism, the Deoband Ulama wanted to develop the "love for political freedom." As they were staunch defenders of Islam and opponents of modernist trends, they had a very important role in re-shaping the Indian Muslim society on the fundamentalist lines, and saved the future Muslim generations from accepting a distorted picture of religion which was gathering momentum in view of strong political movements each aligned with an ideology contrary to the spirit of Islam. Their ideas had a long-time bearing on the political, social and religious affairs of the Muslims. They resisted educational modernization and sided with the nationalist forces. All their ulama commanded the confidence and reverence of the Muslim community.

The British government responded to this in a severe way. As the majority of the Muslims, both ulama and ordinary men, hated the British and everything that smacked of the British culture and state-craft, the British explained that this was, "because of pride of race and feelings of aristocracy."[15] So the British reprisals against the Deoband Ulama was very severe. Many of them were hanged or deported to the Andamans. Their huge properties were confiscated.

In 1866, these ulama, after the decision taken by a board, established the Deoband Seminary at Deoband in U.P. This was a first step towards a fundamentalist venture. Among its founders were Muhammad Qasim Nanawtiwi and Rasheed Ahmad Gangohi. The seminary worked according to a new programme based on the experience of the disaster at Balakot (1831) and the Pathan resistance to the Implementation of pure Islam.[16] And a keen observer like Hunter could not fail to detect the potential threat of this planning, for his government.[17] Therefore to avert the situation and to save the government from any future problems, Hunter in his book pleaded for a more realistic policy to be adopted by the government which had been creating enemies all around. In this context he showed with facts and figures that Muslims were being discriminated against everywhere and it was necessary to follow a more lenient policy towards them, in order to win them to their side.

Simultaneously at work with the Deoband school of thought was the Aligarh School of thought with a similar objective but a different strategy. The leader of this school was Sayyed Ahmed Khan (1817-1898), a religiously brought up Muslim. Despite his orthodox Muslim upbringing his movement was aimed at popularising British culture, education and administration. This school of thought, with Nawab Abdul Lateef as its worker, exhorted the Muslims to learn the English Language and western sciences in order to develop a favourable attitude towards the British and to secure lucrative job with the English. Upto this time the Ulama had declared the learning of English language a heresy, but Nawab Abdul Lateef said, "If any language in India could lead to the advancement in life ... it is English.[18] Sir Sayed was the leader of this group of Muslims who, in view of the growing loss of the Muslim community at the hands of the British had decided to change the course of actions in order to improve the community's political, social, economic and educational conditions. The British tirade against the Muslims hurt him. So he mobilized the opinion of the masses in order to sumbit their loyalties to the British to secure long-term favourable effects.

Sayyid Ahmed Khan studied the entire political and social situation, and arrived at the conclusion that if Muslims were to be able to survive they should be friendly to the British. The British Government had developed a dislike for the Muslim Ulama, so in an Urdu pamphlet[19] written by him in 1859, Sayyid Ahmed Khan, made a plea for a correct assessment of the Muslims and their position vis-a-vis the government. He said that though Muslims were wrong in being hostile to the British some of the measures of the British rulers themselves encouraged such a difference in the Muslim attitude.[20] He made a reference to the British rulers' studied connivance at the collection of arms and soldiers by the Muslims in the 1820s for a Jehad against the Sikhs. He also cited some instances where the Mujahideen under Sayyid Ahmed Barelvi received direct help from the administrative machinery.[21] Though the Muslims have also blundered in being anti-British, Sir Sayed argued, all hope was not lost and the Muslims could even now be won back with the help of a prudent policy.

Sir Sayed with his typical utilitarian attitude wanted a very cordial relationship between the British and the Muslims. He learnt from experience that for Muslims to prosper and to be on equal terms with the Hindus, they should maintain good relationship with their British rulers. Contrary to the Deoband school of thought, the Aligarh School was committed to educational modernization for the socio-economic rehabilitation of the Muslims.

Sir Sayed Ahmed Khan, in his anxiety to please the British often went out of the way also. Though he sincerely wanted to remove the backwardness of the Muslim society through English education, his measures often turned out to be countrary to the spirit of Islam. This brought him the distrust of the people he was working so hard for.

It was part of his movement, launched in favour of the British culture that Sir Sayed started schools and translation societies for translating English books on various subjects into Urdu. Then he published his own commentary on the Bible.[22] He started pleading with the Indian Muslims for better understanding of the Christians who were, also "the people of the Book"[23] (Ahal-e-kitab).

In 1863 he founded an institution called the scientific society to translate scientific, literary and historical English works into Urdu and to publish them so that the Muslims who hated English education could realize the merits of the British culture.[24] The society started a journal, 'Institute gazette', in 1866 to make the Indians familiar with the English form of government and to cultivate in them political thinking and intellectual capacity.[25] This was followed by the establishment of a new organization called the British Indian Association consisting of Hindu and Muslim landlords and the British officers in the province, in order to increase contact between them for better understanding of the British culture and administration. In 1861 he published a pamphlet, "The Loyal Muhamadans of India", and described the loyal deeds of Muslim landlords and princes who had assisted the East India Company in putting down the 1857 revolt.[26] Then Sir Sayed launched a campaign against the social weaknesses of the Indians. For this purpose he started a journal in Urdu, *Tahzibul-Akhlaq* (1869) which, in a lucid style and language pleaded for social reforms in the Muslim society. Without considering whether his pleas went against the teachings of Islam, Sir Sayyid made appeals to Muslim masses for "giving up of Purdah by the Muslim women, adoption of western culture and English education, and acceptance of women's education etc."[27] He started collecting funds for the Muhammadan Anglo-Oriental College, Aligarh. The modernist Muslim and Hindu Zamindars, the British hobbles and the loyalist Princes contributed liberally. The Aligarh College was finally established in 1875 with an English Principal.

As if to cap all his pro-British measures, Sir Sayyid started writing a new commentary on the Quran for a modern interpretation of the Book, with a view to accelerate the adoption of modern ideas. On the basis of his new interpretation of the Quran he made out a case for his reforms.[28] He said the Quran had to be understood on the basis of reason.[29] For all practical purposes he rejected the Hadith (Traditions of Prophet Muhammad) and Fiqh (Islamic Jurisprudence) on the ground that the two were relevant to the society a thousand years ago and were no longer valid.[30] Thus he tried to develop a totally new interpretation of Islam, not authenticated by Hadith and tradition but assisted by reason and argument.

1.2.3 Effects of the British Socio-cultural Discrimination on the Muslims

The English East India Company, by the end of the 18th century had shifted its chief interest from trade to 'ruling for profit'. The company found that tax-collection would be more profitable than commerce and trade. And the turning point came with Lord Clive's treaty with the Nawab of Bengal in 1765.

Since the beginning of the British colonialism in India, it was with the Muslims that the British had all their dealings, agreements, treaties and covenants. When the British defeated Tipu Sultan on the battlefield in Trichnapally (1790), it was because some of the Muslim traitors had joined hands with the English, in return for favours done to them.

Later, in the Revolt of 1857 the British, taking a distorted view of the situation found that it was the Muslims who had initiated and carried on the course of the Revolt. W.W. Hunter's tirade against the Muslims in his book *The Indian Mussalmans* (1870) makes this clear. Hunter's thesis is that had it not been for the Mussalmans, India could have been won over long time back[31]. This belief was strengthened with the fact that after the Revolt the Indians had tried to restore Bahadur Shah a Muslim, to the throne of Delhi. This increased the British distrust of the Muslims and henceforth the British adopted a well-planned scheme of excluding Muslims from administrative offices, not giving them higher posts, confiscating their properties and, last but not least, keeping them in constant antagonism with their countrymen so that their opinion got divided and their loyalty submerged.

Our endeavour in this chapter is to look at the impact of the British rule on the Muslims against the background of their inherent indifference towards them.

It is not an easy task to describe the nature of the British impact on the Indian Muslims. Basically there were two groups at the Muslim community — the nationalist (pan-Islamic) and the loyalist — corresponding to the teachings of the two major schools of thought of the 19th century — namely the Deoband and the Aligarh. While the Deoband school had aversion for everything that smacked of British culture and tradition, the Aligarh school embraced everything British as a mark of position and status. But it is a fact that the Muslim society got divided into these two major groups only at a later stage. In the very beginning there was a feeling of aversion for the British in the entire Muslim community, soon after the British took over. There were historical and religious reasons for this. Though a number of Hindu Kingdoms had emerged during the period of the dissolution of the Mughul Empire after Aurangazeb, the Muslims could not give up the feeling that they comprised the ruling community in India. So they were hostile to the British whom they accused of ex-propriating them of their political power[32]. The anti-Muslim policy of the British Government after the 1857 revolt, intensified the anti-British feeling of the Muslims. This made the Muslims avoid any contact with the new culture and education which the British introduced in India. They tried to avoid coming under the influence of that education and clung with greater tenacity to the teachings of Islam.

The Muslims developed hostility towards the British also because the impoverishment of the Muslims during the process of the British conquest of India took place at a rapid rate. Many of the finer arts and skilled industrial arts of India had been in the hands of the Muslims and they were thoroughly ruined by the fiscal policy of the East India Company.[33]

Prior to the British, the higher posts in the army, in the civil administration, and in the other higher professions had been in the Muslims' hands. But, with the advent of the British many of the higher and middle-class Muslims were reduced to beggary. Their properties were confiscated through Cornwallis' 'permanent settlement'.[34] There is no doubt therefore that the Muslim mind at the beginning of the 19th century entertained the deepest distrust of the British, who had destroyed their power, and of western education and culture which was associated with the British.[35]

It was only by the end of the 19th century that the Muslims began to take to modern education, and gradually an intelligentsia trained in modern education came into being. The more progressive elements among the Muslims steadily evolved a modern outlook and took the road of political and democratic reform in socio-cultural matters.

1.3 A SEPARATE HOMELAND FOR THE MUSLIMS: THE GENESIS OF PAKISTAN

Culture occupies a very important place in the life of every community. It is through culture that civilizations are formed. And through civilization history is made. If culture is overrun and civilization destroyed, then the community gets wiped off from the pages of history. Hence the importance of culture.

Culture abounds all the subjective and objective manifestations of the life of the people at the individual as well as the collective level. The language, the social order, the ethical code, the political manouvering, the religious beliefs and practices, the customs, traditions, dress, intellectual tastes and aspirations all come under the blanket term 'culture'. And language is the common medium that works as soil for the flourishing of culture.

"Alter the dress and language of the people, you can alter the whole culture,"[36] said Ibn Taimiyah (1263-1328) the great Muslim scholar. History proves the truth of the saying. Once the English education was introduced in India through Lord Macaulay's Minute of the Indian Education', in 1835, India was implicitly annexed to the list of the British colonies. With the introduction of English language in Indian institutions, the socio-political system, the scientific and technological developments and the cultural traits of the Indians underwent a drastic change with the result that all the avenues of human life were westernized in a course of time.

Cultural slavery on principle seems to be far more harmful than political servitude for the cultural survival and indentity of the people. Yet in practice, cultural slavery is not only intimately linked to political slavery but to all intents and purposes they are virtually inseparable. Closely allied with the political slavery is the economic slavery as well.[37]

All the Muslim religious and political leaders who guided the Muslim community in those confused years of the freedom struggle began to worry about how to protect the cultural identity of the Muslim community in India. What would become of the Indian Muslims under native-rule, when the British would have quit and gone? was their query. How would India accommodate all the opposing, divergent cultures, without an absolute power to bring them into harmony with each other? These questions had ultimately left them confused.

There had been constant thinking and rethinking in the entire Muslim community about how to protect its glorious past and ensure its sound future, now that it had virtually lost its political hold in the sub-continent. In the beginning, absolute cultural and political autonomy was the silent demand of the whole community. In this planning and retrospection lay the genesis of the two-nation theory, which aimed at preserving the Muslim cultural heritage, and which eventually paved the way for the demand of a separate homeland.

The idea of a separate land for the Muslims had once been propounded by Sir Sayed Ahmed Khan in 1888 and thereafter Moulana Muhammad Ali also suggested it.[38] Iqbal, (1876-1938) the great Muslim philosopher and spiritual mentor too suggested it very emphatically. In the course his presidential address at the twenty-first session of the All India Muslim League at Allahabad on 29th December, 1930. Iqbal said: "It cannot be denied that Islam, regarded as an ethical ideal plus a certain kind of polity — by which I mean a social structure, regulated by a specific ethical ideal — has been the chief formative factor in the life history of the Muslims of India. It has furnished those basic emotions and loyalties which gradually unify scattered individuals and groups and finally transform them into a well-defined people possessing a moral consciousness of their own... Is it possible to retain Islam as an ethical ideal and to reject it as a polity in favour of national politics in which the religious attitude is not permitted to play any part? This question becomes of special importance in India where the Muslims happen to be in a minority."[39]

Iqbal visualized a separate Muslim state which would simultaneously serve the best interests of India as well as of Islam and would remove internal tensions and stabilise peace and security in India. He observed: "The religious order of Islam is organically related to the social order which it has created. The rejection of the one will eventually involve the rejection of the other. Therefore the construction of a polity on Indian national lines, if it means a displacement of the Islamic principles of solidarity, is simply unthinkable to a Muslim."[40]

In comparing the concept of Islamic solidarity as a social unity with the modern western concept of a nation, Iqbal had taken his cue from Ernest Renan, the French political theorist, who had pointed out that the concept of nationalism was something new and a product of modern western history. Iqbal assimilated Renan's argument in his own political thought, applying it to the Indian situation. Judged by this standard the Hindu-Muslim political complex cannot be defined as constituting a single nationhood, he said. Iqbal also observed that in the past the two communities were divided against one another. There was no clear indication of any will to merge their identities in the future. And by this standard Muslim India constituted a nation by itself[41].

According to Iqbal, the emotional and psychological homogeneity which inspires the will to create a nation does not exist in the subcontinent. It might have been achieved if the administrative and social eclecticism of Akbar or the mystic syncreticism of Kabir had succeeded in catching the imagination of the vast masses of India. Instead these experiments shrivelled into syncreticisms because of their rejection by the great religious grouping and by the caste structure of Hindu society. The fact of diversity within the Indian nation has therefore to be recognized. Ignoring it can only lead to inner tensions. Its recognitions may well lead to cooperation between its two major communities[42].

Iqbal, with his deep insight into things was very much conscious of the position of the Muslims as a minority, and from that standpoint he sought for the best possible solution he could envisage for India's situation. He said that for the Muslims, culture was of much greater consequence in India, and that no political device, however subtle, would make the Indian Muslims lose sight of their cultural identity[43]. He consistently opposed the composite nationalism of the Congress, and in the course of his presidential address at the League's session in 1932, he distinguished between nationalism and patriotism, which according to him had a place in the moral beliefs of man. But, he added, "that which really matters is a man's faith, his culture, his historical traditions. These are the things, which in my eyes are worth living and dying for."[44]

This was a significant pronouncement, unapologetically forecasting the 'two-Nation theory', which had been vaguely suggested by Sayed Ahmad Khan and Maulana Muhammad Ali earlier, and was finally developed by Jinnah.

During 1936-37, Iqbal and Jinnah came into very close

contact politically. In a series of letters to Jinnah, Iqbal pressed the view that the creation of a separate Muslim state was the only feasible solution for the Muslims and for peace in India. He suggested that Jinnah should organize the Muslims to achieve the object in the form of a separate state.

Among other who forcefully propounded theories of a separate homeland for the Muslims was one Dr. Sayyid Abdul Lateef, Secretary of the Muslim Cultural Society of Hyderabad. In 1938 Dr. Lateef wrote an article captioned *The Cultural Future of India*. The main theme of this pamphlet was that India lacked that, "common moral consciousness permeating the life of the entire body of people, who would love to live together as a nation."[45] According to Dr. Sayyid Abdul Lateef, Islam was a 'monotheistic democracy' which, for the sake of uniting humanity removed all barriers of colour, language race and geography. Whereas Hinduism was a 'federation of religions and cultures, a social imperialism, holding under its powerful grip, people standing at every stage of intellectual development'[46]. He said that India is torn between the cultural assertiveness of the Hindus and Muslims and Linguistic provincialism prevails everywhere. Dr. Lateef brushed aside the earlier joint living of the Hindus and the Muslims in the past as close neighbours for centuries in the varied spheres of Indian life[47].

It may be mentioned here that the Congress, through its resolution on fundamental rights, passed at the Karachi session in 1931, guaranteed civil and cultural rights to every unit, individual or communal, of the people of India. Dr. Lateef regarded these safeguards as 'a denial of the organic unity' of India. And he argued: "Religion, personal law and culture cover most of the major fields of life's activity — the spiritual, the social, the economic, the educational (or the intellectual, moral and aesthetic), and in the case of the Muslims, professedly, the political as well. It is governed by their all-embracing code of law called the *Shariat*. Under the promises made by the Congress, ... with cultural safeguards conceded to the Muslims, and in like manner to the Hindus, Christians and others, what really gets established is a federation of culturally autonomous nationalities and not a single nationality."[48]

The main difference between Dr. Lateef's concept of division and that of the Muslim League was that the former wanted a federation of culturally autonomous states — i.e., a zonal plan of having India as 'a single political entity i.e., a single federation comprising culturally autonomous states'. Whereas the Muslim league insisted that 'the Pakistan states should remain in isolation and should have no constitutional relation with the rest of India.'[49]

During the Round Table Conference held in London in 1930 and 1931, Jinnah's doubts about the prospects of the Muslims receiving a fair deal from the Congress became visible. As hostility between the Congress and the League depend between 1937 and 1939, the Muslim, and Jinnah, as their Principal leader. When the Government of India Act of 1935 was passed, dividing India into federations of Muslims and Hindus, with a central federal government to supervise, Jinnah opposed it. He said that the problem in India was not inter-communal; it was inter-national and had to be so treated. So long as this fact was not recognized, any constitution imposed on unwilling ethnic components would lead to disaster. The only course open to us all is to allow the major nations separate homelands by dividing India into autonomous national states. For, (with this division) the rivalry and natural desire and efforts on the part of one to dominate the social order and establish political supremacy over the other, in the government of the country will disappear[50].

The course of the Second World War made it clear that the British rule would end at the termination of the war. The influential Muslim politicians in India who had an Independent Muslim nation before them as a goal were only waiting for a proper time to get their demand sanctioned.

In the meantime the British Government too gave utmost encourage to the idea of division, though very covertly.

A proper constitutional body was required by the Indian Muslims to pursue the demand for Pakistan to the end. The Muslim League which claimed to be the sole representative of the Muslims of the subcontinent, was assigned the task of supering the demand. And the League gradually advanced for its previous demands of separate electorates and special weightages, to that of a separate sovereign Muslims state. The politico-ideological basis for the demand was the two-nation theory, propounded by Sir Sayed Ahmed Khan and Moulana Mohammad Ali.

According to the two-Nation theory, the Muslims, a socio-religious category dispersed all over India — were a distinct nation entitled to acquire a separate geographical area. They were entitled to occupy a definite territory because they had a common religion, a common cultural background, a common heritage and a common psychological make-up. In his address to the Lahore session of the league in 1940, Jinnah declared that the Indian Muslims were a distinct nations, and therefore, it would be absurd to thrust a common constitution and a common social order for them, as for the non-Muslims. He argued: "It is extremely difficult to appreciate why our Hindu friends fail to understand the real nature of Islam and Hinduism. They are not simply two religions but two distinct social orders."[51]

To refute the argument of the geographical unity of India, Jinnah quoted a number of historical precedents. He said: "India never was one, never was a nation, never was a country governed by one single power even with the sword. It is a sub-continent of different nationalities and peoples. It was never governed in history by one single power. Even today when constitutionally and legally Britain is ruling over India, one third (of it) is not British. This administrative oneness is entirely the making of the British ... Its sanction is the British bayonet, and not the sanction of the peoples."[52]

It was thus a common decision of the leading Muslim leaders in the country that it was absolutely essential in the interests of an abiding peace of the vast Indian sub-continent and in the interests of unhampered cultural developments, the economic and social betterment and political self-determination of the two Nations — the Hindus and the Muslims, that India be partitioned into two separate states.

The British attitude was also clear by now. They wanted to divide and quit. The only difficulty before them was how to put their plan into action without gaining the ill-will of the vast majority who were against partition. To accomplish their evil design, the Britishers took a shrewd step. They followed the ingenious course of putting forward such schemes before the congress as would appear very disastrous, so that the Congress could be made to agree to the less disastrous one.

Finally, when the Congress came forward to accept partition, it had the choice between (i) a so-called united India with a weak centre with hundreds of autonomous Indian states dotted all over, and a sword perpetually hanging on its unity, (ii) and on the other hand the division of India into two sovereign states — the Indian Union and the Pakistan.[53]

On 3 June 1947, the Congress and the Muslim League accepted Lord Mountbatten's plan for partitioning India into India and Pakistan.

But the Muslim state did not come very easily. It came with a communal holocaust of the worse kind on both sides of the new borders. Millions were killed and many millions were uprooted. Not even quarter of the population could migrate to their respective lands. The most experienced Muslim political organizations were rooted in Indian rather than in Pakistan. Indian Muslim politicians, who went to Pakistan, lost all their reputation and became men of dwindling appeal. Political life did not develop in the new state; institutions and administration remained as they were in British India. Shariat Laws were hardly enforced cultural prejudices were at their highest and in the course of time the internal social and linguistic prejudices, lack of unity among those at the helm of political affairs, absence of proper statesmanship and acute political short-sightedness forced the eastern wing of Pakistan into secession as an autonomous state of Bangladesh in 1969. This was the eventual plight of the so-called Islamic state, whether or not its founders makers approve of it.

Now if one looks back in retrospection at the sophisticated ideal, the high hopes, the political strategy, the wishful thinking and the years of planning that went into the creation of the state of Pakistan, the entire process, even to the present day seems to have been a big farce. With the present State of Pakistan (except for the recent attempts at Islamisation) having come up on the international political horizon as yet another nation-State, all the dreams of the founders remain shattered and unfulfilled. Going through the record of the comments made by the Muslim League leaders themselves after they settled in Pakistan, it seemed that they had themselves begun to harbour doubts about what they had done and wanted to do[54]. It would probably require another quarter of a century for the country to get over its internal socio-political chaos and to begin a fresh attempt at consolidation of the Islamization which had recently set in/been launched.

1.4 THE AFTERMATH OF PARTITION (1947)

The most numerous religious group in India after the Hindus, is the Muslims, who make up about tenth of the population even after the partition of the predominantly Muslims states of Sind and Punjab into Pakistan. The Muslims have a history of over twelve hundred years in India. They are an ineradicable part of India's history and culture. India has gained much, and has more to gain from its Muslim population. The Muslims were said to be a very strong force against the British. Tipu was a force to be reckoned with. When it was impossible for the British to subvert him, traitors were employed to defeat this valiant son of India. There are many more examples of major roles played by patriotic Indians against any foreign force.

To the utter disadvantage of the Muslims India was partitioned. The Muslim community cannot be held responsible for it. It was a mixed leadership of the Congress and the Muslims which fostered the plan. It was also very much a part of the age-old British policy of divisiveness that brought about the partition. The pan-Islamic, Deoband School of thought to which most Muslims subscribe never accepted the theory of partition of

India, even to this day. The Deoband school of thought rejected the two-nation theory or the demand for a separate homeland as undesirable much less Islamic or favourable to the Muslims in India from either political, social or economic points of view. The responsibility of the preservation of cultural heritage and Islamic identity of the community could never be put on the shoulders of such irresponsible and secular minded leaders whose lives showed no traces of the impact of Islam and who were pitifully unaware of the Islamic tenets. This school of thought was convinced that a separate state was not enough to protect the distinctive socio-cultural identity and religious status of a community or people. Rather such a protection demanded complete freedom to maintain not only its identity as a separate entity but also to extend its message to the fellow countrymen. And this could be possible only in the united India under a secular constitution, in the truest sense of the word.

The partition of the country has brought many disadvantages to the Indian Muslim community. The migration of the Muslims of India into the so-called Muslim land of Pakistan left the Indian Muslims with the stigma of disloyalty for no fault of theirs. The Muslims who were just a minority before Independence became second grade citizens, with the minority status further enhanced (1/10 at present) — without any dynamic leadership of their own, left at the mercy of the majority, community always begging for protection of their rights, for grant of privileges, for proportionate representation in Grade I and II services and thus exposing themselves as a group of people always weeping and sobbing either for some injustice done to them or in advance for a likely unjust treatment.

REFERENCES

1. H.K. Shervani, *Cultural Trends in Medieval India*, Bombay, 1968, p. 3.
2. Ibid.
3. Amalendu, De, *Roots of Separatism in Nineteenth Century Bengal*, Calcutta, 1974, p. 4.
4. Amalendu, De, *Islam in Modern India*, Maya Prakashan, Calcutta, 1982, p. 11.

5. Nizami, K.A., "Socio-Religious Movements in Indian Islam" (1863-1898), from *India and Contemporary Islam,* editor S.T. Lokhandwalla, Simla, 1971, pp. 107-108.
6. Kaur, Uma, *Muslims and Indian Nationalism,* Manohar Publications, 1977, p. 4.
7. Ibid., p. 3.
8. Ibid., p. 4.
9. Desai, A.R. *Social Background of Indian Nationalism,* Popular Prakashan, Bombay, p. vii (from the Introduction).
10. Ibid., p. viii.
11. Maazzam, Anwar, "The Indian Muslim: A Dilemma of the Dual Personality", in *India and Contemporary Islam,* ed. S.T. Lokhandwalla, Indian Institute of Advanced Study, Simla, 1971, pp. 196-197.
12. Ahmad, Aziz, *Islamic Modernism in India and Pakistan* (1957-1964), Oxford University Press, London, 1967, p.104.
13. Ibid.
14. Amalendu, De, *Islam in Modern India,* Maya Prakashan, Calcutta, 1982, p.13.
15. Hunter, W.W. *The Indian Musalmans,* London, 1870, p. 26.
16. Karandikar, M.A. *Islam in India's Transition to Modernity,* Orient Longman, Bombay, 1969, p.143.
17. Ibid.
18. Wilfred Cantwell Smith, *Modern Islam in India,* London, Victor Gollantz Ltd., 1946, p.106.
19. Sayyid Ahmed Khan, *Asbab-e-Baghawate Hind,* Delhi, 1859, p. 5.
20. Karandikar, M.A., *Islam in India's Transition to Modernity,* Orient Longman, Bombay, 1969, p. 139.
21. Ibid., p.140.
22. Ibid.
23. Ibid.
24. Ibid.
25. Ibid.
26. Ibid.
27. Ibid., p. 143.
28. Ibid.

29 Ibid.

30 Ibid.

31. Ibid. p. 143

32. Desai, A.R. "Communalism — Its Real Essence", in *Social Background of Indian Nationalism*, Popular Prakashan, Bombay, 1970, p. 299.

33. Ibid., p. 300.

34. Ibid.

35. Ibid.

36. Ibe-Taimiyah, *Islami aur Ghair Islami Tahzeeb*, Academy of Islamic Research and Publications, Luckhnow, 1966, p. 67.

37. Jameelah, Maryam, *Islam and Modernism*, Mohammad Yusuf Khan (Publishers), Sant Nagar, Lahore, W. Pakistan, 1975, p. 32.

38. Penderel, Mooh, *Divide and Quit*, pp.11-12.

39. Iqbal, Muhammad, Struggle for Independence, pp.12-15, from *Mazameen* (Urdu), Hyderabad, 1941.

40. Ahmed, Aziz, *Islamic Modernism in India and Pakistan* (1857-1965) Oxford University Press, London, 1967, p. 161.

41. Iqbal, Muhammad, "Struggle for Independence," pp.15-16, from *Mazameen* (Urdu), Hyderabad, 1941, and Ahmed, Aziz, *Islamic Modernism in India and Pakistan (1857-1965)*, Oup: London, 1967, p.162.

42. Allan, G., *Pakistan Movement — Historic Documents*, Published by the Dacca Institute of Research, University of Dacca, Pakistan, 1952.

43. Karandikar, M.A., *Islam in India's Transition to Modernity*, Orient Longman, Bombay, 1969, p. 237.

44. Mitra, Annual Register, pp. 48-49.

45. Amalendu, De., *Islam in Modern India*, Maya Prakashan, Calcutta, 1982, p.105.

46. Ibid.

47. Yar Yung, *Pakistan Issue*, pp. 24-25.

48. Ahmad Aziz, *Islamic Modernism in India and Pakistan (1857-1965)* Oup: London, 1967, p.165. And *Speeches and Writings of Mr. Jinnah*, Presidential Address to Lahore, 1940 Session of the Muslim League, Pub. Qaid-e-Azam University, W. Pakistan.

49. A.R. Desai, *Social Background of Indian Nationalism*, Popular Prakashan, Bombay, p. 407.

50. Ibid., p. 415.

51. *Speeches and Writings of Mr. Jinnah*. Speech at the Meeting of the Muslim

League Council, Delhi, November 9, 1940, Pub. Qaid-e-Azam Univ., W. Pakistan.

52. Karandikar, M.A. *Islam in Transition to Modernity*, Orient Longman, Bombay, 1969, p. 245.

53. Akbar, M.J. "Jinnah Sold the Birthright of the India Muslim for a Bowl of Soup", *The Illustrated Weekly of India*, ed. Pritish Nandy, Dec. 30-Jan. 5, 1985, from an article on Communalism in the forthcoming book: *India: A Siege Within,* to be published by the Penguin Books as part of their Golden Jubilee List.

BIBLIOGRAPHY

A. COMPARATIVE RELIGION

Askari, Syed Hasan
Collected works of Prof. Sayed Hasan Askari. Patna, Khuda Bakhsh Oriental Public Library, 1985.

Inter-religion: A collection of essays. Aligarh, Printwell Publications, 1977.

Cole, W. O.
Sikkhism and its Indian Context 1469-1708: the attitude of Guru Nanak and early Sikhism to Indian religious beliefs and practices (includes Muslim context and Guru Nanak's attitude to Hinduism and Islam). London, Darton, Longman and Todd, 1984.

Dara Shikuh, Muhammad
Majma ul-Bahrain or the mingling of the two oceans. Edited in the Original Persian with English translation by H. Mahfuz ul-Haq. Calcutta, Asiatic Society, 1982.

Dehlvi, Mohammad Saeed
Izabella: A unique book of its kind for comparative study of Islam and Christianity. Tr. from Urdu by Rahim Ali al-Hashmi. Delhi, Dini Book Depot, 1974.

Devadason, E. D.
Study on conversion and its aftermath. Madras, C. L. S. 1982.

Durrany, K. S.
Religion in society: selected Indian press index of comparative religion. New Delhi, Uppal Pub. House, 1983.

Ghai, O. P.
Unity in diversity: A guide to the understanding of the fundamental unity underlying the great living religions. London, Skilton, 1986.

Hedayatullah, Muhammed
Kabir, the apostle of Hindu-Muslim unity: interaction of Hindu-Muslim ideas in the formation of the bhakti movement with special reference to Kabir the bhakta. Delhi, Motilal B., 1977.

Hick, O. and Hasan Askari ed.
Experience of religious diversity. Aldershot, Gower, 1985.

Nadvi, Abdul Hasan A.
Appreciation and interpretation of the religion in the modern age. Lucknow, Academy of Islamic Research and Pub., 1982.

Roy Chaudhuri, M.L.
Din-i-Ilahi, or the religion of Akbar. New Delhi, Oriental Reprint, 1985.

Samad, Ulfat Aziz us,
Comparative Study of Christianity and Islam. Delhi, Noor Pubs. 1986.

Sandeela, F.M.
Islam, Christianity and Hinduism. Delhi, Taj & Co., 1983.

Troll, Christian W.
Islam in India: studies and commontaries, V. 1: Akbar: mission and miscellaneous studies. Sahibabad, Vikas, 1982.

B. RELIGIOSITY

Ahmed, C.N.
Religion of Islam. Calicut, Azad Book Stall, 1979.

Ahmad, Imtiaz.
Ritual and religion among Muslims in India. New Delhi, Manohar Publications, 1982.

Ali, A Yusuf.
Message of Islam. New Delhi, Kitab Bhavan, 1987.

Ali, Maulana Muhammed.
Religion of Islam. New Delhi, S. Chand. 1983.

Ansari, G. Gani.
Who is a Muslim? Hyderabad, The Author, 1973.

Ansari, Sabihuddin Ahmed, Tr.
Lessons of Islam. (Talim ul Islam). Delhi, Kutub Khane Azizia, 1983.

Ashfaq, Ahmed and Ahmed Saeed Khan,
Religion: A bibliography. Aligarh, Centre of West Asian Studies and Institute of Islamic Studies, 1970.

Carpenter, J. Estlin.
Theism in medieval India. Delhi, Orient Book 1977 (rpt).

Dehlvi, Abdul Huqq Mohaddith.
Perfection of faith. Lahore : Islamics International, 1987. (Rept)

Engineer, Asghar Ali.
Islam in South and South East Asia. Delhi, Ajanta, 1985.

Esposito, J.L.
Islam in Asia: religion, politics and society. New York, OUP, 1987.

Faruqi, Burhan Ahmed

Friedmann, Y. ed.
Islam in Asia: South Asia. V.1. Westview, 1984.

Fyzee, Asaf A.A.
Modern approach to Islam. New Delhi, OUP, 1981.

Hameed, H. Abdul.
Islam at a glance. New Delhi, Vikas, 1981.

Hamidullah, Muhammad.
Introduction to Islam. Qum: Ansariyan, 1982.

Islam: A General Picture. Hyderabad, Saifuddin Literary Trust, 1979.

Iqbal, Muhammad.
Shikwa and Jawab-i-Shikwa: Complaint and Answer: Iqbal's dialogue with Allah. Tr. Kushwant Singh. Delhi OUP, 1981.

Iqbal, Sheikh M.
Mission of Islam. New Delhi. Taj and Co., 1983.

Realms of Peace. Delhi. Idarah-i Adabiyat-i Delhi, 1979.

Iqbal, Sheikh Mohammad and Sheikh Talal Javed Iqbal.
Ideals of Islam & Other essays. Delhi. Idarah-i Adabiyat-i Delhi. 1982 (IAD Religion-Philosophy Series, 12).

Islahi, M. Sadruddin.
Building up the foundation of the faith. Delhi. Crescent Pub. Co., 1982.

Kashmiri, Aziz.
Christ in Kashmir. Srinagar, J & K. Roshni Pub., 1988.

Kifayatullah, Mufti M.
Lessons in Islam. Delhi. Kutub Khana Azizia, 1982.

Kremer, A. F. Von.
Islamic Studies. Tr. J.S. Khuda Bukhsh. Lahore, Sind Sagar Academy, 1974.

Mujahid, Abdul Malik.
Conversion to Islam: Untouchables strategy of protest. Chambersburg, PA; Anima Pub, 1989.

Nadvi, Abdul Hasan A.
From the depth of the heart in America. Tr. M.A. Kidwai. Lucknow, Academy of Islamic Research and Publications, 1978.

Guide book of Muslims. Lucknow, Academy of Islamic Research and Publications, 1985.

Islam — the perfect religion. Lucknow, Academy of Islamic Research, 1979.

Islam in changing world. Lucknow, Academy of Islamic Research, 1976.

Speaking plainly to the West. Lucknow, Academy of Islamic Research, 1979.

Nomani, Muhammed Manzoor.
Islamic faith and practice. Lucknow, Academy of Islamic Research, 1982.

What Islam is. Lucknow, Academy of Islamic Research, 1979.

Qureshi, Ishtiaq H.
Religion of peace. New Delhi. Kitab Bhavan, 1988.

Rogers, Michael.
Spread of Islam. New Delhi. OUP., 1976.

Rose, H.A.
Religious history of Islam., Delhi, National Book Shop, 1986.

Saiyidain, K.G.
Islam, the religion of peace. New Delhi, Islam and the Modern Age Society, 1976.

Samuel, M. Zwemer.
Islam: A challenge to faith. New Delhi. Star Pub. 1986.

Sharma, S.R.
Religious policy of the Mughal emperors. Bombay. Asia, 1974.

Siddiqi, A. Hameed.
Islam and the remaking of humanity. Delhi. Islamic Book Trust, 1982.

What Islam gave to humanity, Delhi. Crescent Pub. Company, 1981.

Siddiqi, M. Iqbal.
Humanity at the death's door. Delhi, International Islamic Publications, 1987.

Valiuddin, Mir.
Essential features of Islam. Hyderabad. Dairat ul-Maarif Press, 1970.

Islamic monotheism. Delhi, Idarsh-i Adabiyat-i Delli, 1978.

Waliyullah, Shah.
Sataat. Tr. G.N. Jalbani. New Delhi. Kitab Bhavan, 1981.

Al-Budur-al-Bazighah. English tr. by G.N. Jalbani. Islamabad, Natiional Hijra council, 1985.

Wingate, Andrew; et al
Tamilnadu conversions to Islam. Bangalore, Christian Inst. for the Study of Religion and Society, 1982.

Zakaria, Ahmed B.

This is Islam. Bombay, Islamic Cultural Centre, 1988.

C. QURAN

Adil, H.M.
Introduction to Quran. New Delhi. Adam Publications, 1983.

Ahmad, Nisar.
Fundamental Teachings of Quran and Hadith. 2nd. ed. Delhi, Kitab Bhavan, 1984.

Ahmad, S. Barakat.
Introduction to Quranic Script. New Delhi. Macmillan, 1984.

Ali, A. Yusuf.
Holy Quran: Text, Translation and Commentary. New Delhi.

Kitab Bhavan, 1982.

Meaning of the Illustrious Quran (Being a textless edition of the English Translation of the Holy Quran). New Delhi, Kitab Bhavan, 1978.

Ali, Ahmed.
Al- Quran: A contemporary translation, New Delhi. OUP, 1987.

Aneesuddin, Mir.
Index to the Holy Quran. Hyderabad. Islamic Academy of Sciences, 1988.

Binark, I. and H. Eren.
World bibliography of translations of the meanings of the Holy Quran: printed translations, 1515-1980. London. Keagen Paul International, 1987.

Chippa, A. Karim.
Beauty and wisdom of the Holy Quran. 3rd ed. New Delhi. Kitab Bhavan, 1987.

Crollius, A.A Roest.
Word in the experience of revelation, in Quran and Hindu Scriptures. Athens, Univ. of Georgia. Press, 1974.

Daryabadi, A. Majid.
Tafsir -ul-Quran 4v. Lucknow. Academy of Islamic Research and Publications, 1981-1985.

Faruqi, I.H. Azad.
Tarjumanul Quran: A critical analysis of Maulana Abul Kalam Azad's approach to the understanding of the Quran. New Delhi. Vikas, 1982.

Fazluddin.
Dawatul Quran: The Quranic message with interpretation. Tr. S. Mohammed Iqbal. Delhi. Taj & co., 1982.

Husain, Syed Akhtar.
The Message of Quran. Lucknow. Academy of Islamic Research 1977.

Jung, Nizamat.
Approach to the study of the Quran. New Delhi. Kitab Bhavan, 1987.

Khan. M. Muhsin and M. Taqiuddin al-Halali.
Interpretation of the meanings of the Noble Quran. New Delhi. Kitab Bhavan, 1989.

Kheirie, Alhaj Khan Bahadur A.A.
Index-cum-concordance for the holy Quran. New Delhi. Kitab Bhavan, 1988.

Khuda Bakhsh Library
Catalogue of Arabic and Persian manuscripts in Khuda Bakhsh Library. Patna. v. 29. (Quranic Science, Arabic) Patna, 1971.

Latif, S. Abdul.
Mind al-Quran builds. Delhi. Idara-i-Adasiyat-i-Delhi. 1981.

Tarjuman-al-Quran. Hyderabd, Syed Abdul Latif Trust for Quranic Cultural Research, 1980.

Malik, S.K.
Quranic concept of War. New Delhi. Himalayan, 1986.

Munawar, Muhammad.
Iqbal and Quranic wisdom. Delhi. Noor Pub., 1986.

Musleh, Abu Mohammed.
Last part of Holy Quran (Para Aam). New Delhi. Kitab Bhavan, 1979.

Nadvi, Abul Hasan.
Faith Versus Materialism (The message of Surat Ul-Kahaf). Lucknow. Academy of Islamic Research & Publications, 1970.

Nadvi, S. M.
Quran: A historical geography. Delhi. Classicial Pubs. 1968.

Nomani, M. Manzoor
The Quran and you. Lucknow Academy of Islamic Research 1978.

Pickthail, M.M.
Holy Quran: Translation with Arabic text. New Delhi. Kitab Bhavan, 1982.

Pirzada, Shams.
Dawatul Quran. Arabic text, translation and commentary. Tr. A.K. Shaikh. Bombay. Idara Dawatul Quran, 1983.

Rahman, Afzal-ur.
Subject index of the holy Quran. New Delhi. Noor Publishing House, 1987.

Roberts, Robert.
The social laws of the Quran, considered with those of the Hebrew and other ancient codes. New Delhi. Cosmo Publications, 1978.

Shad, Abdul Rehman and Abdul Hameed Siddiqi .
Selections from the holy Quran and the Ahadith. Delhi. Noor Pub, 1986.

Valiuddin, Mir.
Quranic Sufism. Delhi. Motilal Banarsidas, 1977.

D. HADITH

Abu Dawud,
Sunan Abu Dawud. 3 v. Delhi, Al-Madina, 1986.

Sunan. Tr. asnd Notes by Ahmed Hasan. New Delhi. Kitab Bhavan, 1986.

Abul Fazl, Mirza.
Sayings of the Prophet Muhammed. New Delhi. Award Pub. House 1976.

Bukhari, Imam
Sahih al-Bukhari. V.5. Tr. with notes by Mohammed Asad. New Delhi, Kitab Bhavan, 1978.

Sahih al-Bukhari. Tr. M. Mohsin Khan. 9 vols. New Delhi, Kitab Bhavan, 1980

Dehlvi, A Said
Hadees-e-Qudsi: Signs of Allah. Tr. from Urdu by Rahim Ali- al-Hashmi. Delhi, Dini Book Depot, 1972.

Hamidullah, M
Sahifah Hammam Ibn Munnabih. Hyderabad, Habib & Co., 1979

Khuda Bakhsh Library
Catalogue of Arabic and Persian manuscripts in Khuda Bakhsh Library, Patna. V.20 (Traditions:Arabic), Patna, 1970

Malik, Imam
Muwatta. Tr. M. Rahimuddin. New Delhi, Kitab Bhavan, 1981.

Muslim, Imam
Sahih Muslim. Tr. M. Abdul Hamid Siddiqui. 4.v. New Delhi, Kitab Bhavan, 1984.

Nadvi, Abul Hassan
Role of Hadith. Lucknow, Academy of Islamic Research & Publications, 1975.

Nomani, M. Manzoor
Meaning and message of the Traditions. 5.v. Lucknow, Academy of Islamic Research and Publications, 1984

Pirzada, Shams
Jawahirul Hadith or gems of the sayings of the Prophet. Tr. Abdul Karim Shaikh. Bombay, Idara Dawatul Quran, 1987

Shabbir, Mohammed
Authority and authencity of Ahadith as a source of Islamic Law. New Delhi, Kitab Bhavan, 1982.

Waliyullah, Shah
Tawil al-Ahadith. Tr. G N Jalbani. New Delhi, Kitab Bhavan, 1981.

E. PROPHET MUHAMMED

Abbasi, S.M. Madni
Family of the Holy Prophet New Delhi. Adam Pub., 1983.

Ahmed, M.M. Inayat
Authenticated mircales of Muhammad. New Delhi. Award Pub. House, 1982.

Ahmad, S. Barakat
Muhammad and the Jew: A Re-examination. New Delhi. Vikas 1979.

Ahmed, Zahir Mohammed
Glimpses of the Prophet's life and times. New Delhi. Ambika Publications, 1980.

Ali, P. Mohammed
A biography of Prophet Mohammad. (n.p.), The Author, 1982.

Amin, Mohammad
Wisdom of Prophet Mohammad. Delhi. Islamic Book Service, 1987.

Carpenter, Humphrey and Others
Founders of faith. Jesus; The Buddha; Muhammad and Confucius Oxford. Oxford University, 1986.

Dinet, E
The life of Mohammad; the Prophet of Allah. Delhi, Kutab Khana Ishayat-ul-Islam, 1977.

Dods, Marcus
Mohammad, Buddha and Christ: Four lectures on natural and revealed religion. New Delhi. Indological Book House, 1987.

Durrani, M. H.
Muhammad: The Biblical Prophet. New Delhi. Adam, 1986.

Gauba, Khalid Lalif
Prophet of the Desert. New Delhi. Adam Pub., 1981.

Hamidullah, Muhammad
Battlefields of the Prophet Muhammad: A contribution to Muslim Military History. Ed.2. Hyderabad, Habib and Co. 1983.

First written constitution in the world. Hyderabad. Habib & Co., 1983.

Mohammad Rasulullah: A concise survey of the Life and work of the founder of Islam. Hyderabad, Habib and Co., 1974.

The Prophet's establishing a state and his succession. Hyderabad, Habib & Co., 1986.

Haque, Zahurul
Muhammad the greatest leader. New Delhi. Noor Pub. House, 1988.

Hashmi, Rahim Ali.
Mohammad: The benefactor of humanity. Delhi. Board of Islamic. Pub, 1971.

Husain, S. Athar
Prophet Muhammad and his mission. Lucknow. Academy of Islamic Research & Publications, 1978.

Kamaluddin, Khwaja
Ideal Prophet. Delhi, Kalinga Pub., 1987 (rept).

Khan, Sir Syed Ahmed
Essays on the life of the Mohammad and subject subsidiary hitherto. V.I. Delhi, Idara - 1 - Adabiyati Delhi, 1981.

Khan, Wahiddudin
Muhammad: The Prophet of revolution. New Delhi, Islamic Centre Publications, 1986.

Kirmani, Ziauddin
Last Messenger with a lasting message. Delhi, Islamic Book Trust, 1982.

Muir, William
Mohammadan controvesy: biographies of Mohammad, Sprenger on Tradition: the Indian Litrugy and the Psalter. Allahabad, R S. Pub. House 1979.

Nadvi, Abul Hassan Ali
Final Prophet and the perfect religion. Lucknow, Academy of Islamic Research & Pub. 1977

Islamic concept of Prophethood Tr. by Mohiuddin Ahmad Lucknow, Academy of Islamic Research & Pub; 1976

Mercy for the world. Lucknow, Academy of Islamic Research and Publications, 1977.

Muhammad Rasulullah: The Apostle of Mercy. Lucknow, Academy of Islamic Research and Publications, 1982.

Prophet Muhammad in the mirror of his supplications. Lucknow. Academy, 1977

Nadvi, Syed Sulaiman
Mercy of the worlds — Rahmantul-lil-Aa-lameen: life sketch of Prophet Muhammad. Delhi, Dini Book depot, 1977-78. 3 v.

Muhammad: The Ideal Prophet. Tr. Mohiuddin Ahmed. Lucknow, Academy of Islamic Research, 1977

Narayan, R.K.
Mohammad: The Prophet of the Islam: A flame in the Desert. New Delhi, Lancers, 1978

Poonawala, Ismail K.
History of al-tabari, v. 9 Last years of the Prophet. The formation of the State A.D. 630-632, A.H.8-11. New Delhi, Inter India Pub., 1984 (Rpt.)

Qureshi, Sultan A.
Letters of the Holy Prophet. Delhi. Noor Publishing House, 1986.

Rao, K.S. Ramakrishna
Muhammad: The Prophet of Islam. Delhi. Crescent Publishing Co., 1982

Raza, Ali Musa
Muhammad in the Quran. Delhi. Idarah- I-Adabiyat-i-Delhi, 1980.

Saeed, Ahmad
Prophetic medical sciences (The saviour). Tr. Badr Azimabadi. Delhi. Dini Book Depot, 1987.

Salim, M. Kunju
Muhammad and the Rise of Islam. New Delhi. Vikas Bhavan, 1988.

Shad, Abdul Rehman
From Adam to Muhammad. Delhi. Noor Pub., 1986.

Siddiqui, A.H
Life of Muhammad. Calcutta. Hilal Pub, 1982.

Siddiqi, M. Yasin Mazhar
Organization of government under the Prophet. Delhi, Idara-e-Adabiyat-e-Delhi, 1987.

Smith, Bosworth
Mohammad and Mohammedanism. New Delhi. Metropolitan Book Co. (Distributor), 1988.

F. PHILOSOPHY

Fa. General

Chandra, R. B. Harish

Khuda: Quranic Philosophy. New Delhi. Parichay Overseas, 1983.

Khan, Khaja
Philosophy of Islam. New Delhi. Kitab Bhavan, 1981.

Khwaja, Jamal
Quest for Islam: A Philosopher's approach. New Delhi. Allied Publishers, 1971.

Lal, Basant K
Contemporary Indian philosophy. Delhi, Motilal Banarsidass, 1978.

Nadvi, I.M.O.
Muslim thought & its sources. Delhi. Idarah-i-Adabiyat-i-Delhi, 1983. (rpt.)

Rafique, M.
Indian and Muslim Philosophy. New Delhi. Metropolitan Book Co. (Distributor), 1988.

Scharfstein, Ben Ami et al.
Philosophy East/ Philosophy West: A critical comparison of Indian Chinese, Islamic and European Philosophy. Oxford. Basil Blackwell, 1978.

Fb. Ethics

Abbasi, S.M. Madni
Islamic manners. New Delhi. D.K. Pub. & Distributors, 1988.

Ahmad, Maulana S.M.
Islam on moral rights. Tr. M.A.K. Ghauri. London. London Mosque, 1976.

Ali, Syed Nawab
Some moral and religious teachings of Imam al-Ghazali. New Delhi. Kitab Bhavan, 1988.

Ansari, M.A. Haq
Ethical philosophy of Miskawaih. Aligarh (NP), 1974.

Husain, Riaz
Etiquettes of life in Islam. Delhi, Islamic Book Trust, 1982.

Razi, Imam
Ilm al-akhlaq. Tr. M.S.H. Masumi ad.ed. New Delhi, Kitab Bhavan, 1981.

Salim, M. Kunju
Islam: ethics and teachings. New Delhi. Kitab Bhavan, 1989

Shad, Abdul Rehman
Muslim Etiquettes. Delhi. Taj Co., 1982.

Umaruddin, M
Ethical philosophy of al-Ghazzali. 2nd ed. Lahore, Institute of Islamic Culture, 1988.

Fc. Sufism

Ansari, Abdul Huq
Sufism and Shariah: A study of Shaykh Ahmad Sirhindi's effort to reform Sufism. Leicester Islamic Foundation, 1986.

Attar, Fariddudin
Muslim saints and mystics: Episodes from the Tadhkirat al-Auliya.Tr. by A.J. Arberry. New York, Routledge, Chapman & Hall, 1979.

Beg, Mirza W.
Big five of India in Sufism. Ajmer, the Author, 1972.

Behari, Banke
Sufism, mystics and yogis of India. Bombay. Bharatiya, 1970.

Bhattacharya, B.
Deified saints of Bengal — A profile. Calcutta. Indian Publications, 1972.

Danner, V. & W. M. Thackston. Tr.
Ibn Ata 'Allah'. The book of wisdom: Intimate conversations, introd., transl. and notes. London, S.P.C.K., 1979.

Digby, Simon
Encounters with jogis in Indian Sufi hagiography. mimegraphed. London, School of Oriental and African Studies, 1970.

Eaton, R. Maxwell
Sufis of Bijapur, 1300-1700, Social roles of Sufis in medieval India. Princeton. Preinceton University Press, 1978.

Ghosh, Sisirkumar
Mystics as a force for change. Wheaton, Theosophical Publishing House, 1981.

Gilani, A. Qadir
Futuh-al-Ghaib: The revelation of the unseen. Tr. Aftabuddin Ahmad. New Delhi, Kitab Bhavan, 1979.

Hakim, H.E.
Islam and Sufism in the light of theology. (n.p.). Theosophical Islamic Assn., 1975.

Haque, Abdul
Allah-o-Noorus samawat-e-wal-Arz. Patna, Labe Litho Press, 1972.

Hussain, S. Athar
Book of Thousand Lights. Lucknow. Academy of Islamic Research, 1975

Hussaini, S.S. Khusro
Sayyid Muhammad Hussayni-i-Gisudiraz on Sufism. New Delhi. Idarah-i-Adabiyat-i-Delli, 1983.

Iqbal, Sir Muhammad.
Secrets of Collective life, translation of Rumuz-i-bekhudi by A.R. Tariq. Lahore. Islamic Book Serivce, 1977.

Secrets of the Self, a philosophical poem. Transl. by R.A.Nicholson. Afterword by Mulk Raj Anand. New Delhi. Arnold Heinemann, 1978.

Secrets of ego, being a descriptive and comprehensive translation of Allama Iqbal's Asrar-i-Khudi; rendered into English by A.R. Tariq. Lahore. Islamic Book Service, 1977.

Jotwani, Motilal
Sufis of Sindh. New Delhi, Publications Division, Ministry of I. and B. 1986.

Khan, Khaja
Studies in Tasawwuf. Delhi. Idarah-i-Adabiyat-i-Delli, 1978.

Khan, Shamsher Ali
Mahboob-e-Khuda. Beloved of Allah. Tr. M. Masroor Khan Saroha. Delhi. Dini Book Depot, 1980.

Lawrence, Bruce B.
Notes from a distant flute: the extant literature of pre-Mughal Indian Sufism. Tehran. Imperial Iranian Academy of Philosophy, 1978.

An overview of Sufi literature in the Sultanate Period (1206-1526 A.D.) Patna, Khuda Bakhsh Oriental Public Library, 1979.

Nadvi, Abul Hasan A.
Pathway to Madina. Lucknow, Academy of Islamic Research, 1982.

Saviours of Islamic spirit. 3 v. Lucknow, Academy of Islamic Research and Publications, 1972.

Al- Qunawi, Sadruddin
Reflections of the awakened (Mirat Arifin) Tr. S.H. Askari. New York, Methuen, 1987.

Qureshi, Burckhardt R.
Sufi music of India and Pakistan: Sound, context and meaning in Gawwali (studies in Ethnomusicology) Leiden, Brill, 1986.

Rafiqi, Abdul Qaiyum
Sufism in Kashmir from the fourteenth to the sixteenth century. Varanasi, Bharatiya Publishing House, 1975

Rastogi, Tarachand
Islamic Mysticism — Sufism. New Delhi. Sterling, 1982.

Rizvi, S.A. Abbas
History of Sufism in India. 2 v. New Delhi, Munsiram Manoharlal, 1983.

Schimmel, Annemarie.
Pain and grace. a study of two mystical writers of eighteenth century Muslim India. Leiden, Brill, 1976.

Siddiqi, M. Suleman
Bahmani Sufis. New Delhi, Idara-i-Adabiyat-i-Dilli, 1989.

Siddiqi, Majid H
Memories of Sufis written in India, Reference to Kashaf-ul-Mahjub, Siyar-Auliya, Siyar-ul-Arifin. Baroda, Dept. of Urdu, Persian and Arabic, M.S. University, 1979.

Waliyullah, Shah
Sufism and the Islamic traditions: The Lamahat & Sataat. Transl. by G.N. Jalbani and ed. by D.B. Fry. London, Octagon Press, 1980.

G. IBADAT

Ahmed, Moinuddin
Namaz: self-taught and Islamic essentials. New Delhi. Kitab Bhavan, 1988.

Dadarkar, Ahmed Bahauddin
Daily prayer book of Islam. Bombay. Taj Publishers, 1987.

Nadvi, Abdul Hasan. A.
Four Pillars of Islam. Tr. Asif Kidwai. Lucknow. Academy of Islamic Research, 1972.

Nazir, Afdal Ahmad
Haj Guide (Brief description of Haj performace with English translation of Prayers). Calcutta. Darul Eshaat Islamia, 1970.

Nizami, Ashraf F.
Namaz: The Yoga of Islam: An ideal practice for physical fitness mental peace and spiritual bliss. Madras, Taraporevala, 1981.

Rahman, Aziz-Ur
History of Jama Masjid and interpretation of Muslim devotions. Delhi Publications India, 1987.

Rao, K.S. Ramakrishna
Significance of prayer in Islam. Delhi. Idarah-i-Adabiyat-i-Dilli, 1986.

H. POLITICS

H. a. General

Akbar, M.J.
India: A siege within. Harmondsworth, Penguin. 1985.

Aziz, K.K.
Muslims under Congress rule, 1937-1939: A Documentary record. 2 v Delhi, Renaissance Pub. House, 1986.

Cumming, J
Political India, 1823-1932. A comperative survey of a century. London. OUP, 1977

Davis, E .
Press and politics in British Western Punjab, 1836-1947, Delhi. Academic Publication, 1983 .

Dev, B.J. and D.K. Lahiri
Politics and cohesion. Delhi. Mittal Pub., 1985.

Dhami, M.S.
Minority leaders of the Indian political system. New Delhi, Sterling, 1975.

Gopalakrishnan, S.
Political movements in South India, 1914-1929. Madras, New Era Pub. 1981.

Hardy, Peter
Muslims of British India. London, Cambridge Univ. Press, 1972.

Hussain, S.T.
Reflections on Kashmir politics. New Delhi. Metropolitan Book Co. (Distributor), 1987.

Mallick, Azizur Rahman
British policy and the Muslims in Bengal: 1757-1856. 2nd ed. Dacca: Bangla Acad. 1977.

Saxena, V. Kumar. ed
Muslims and the Indian National Congress, 1885-1924. New Delhi. Discovery, 1985.

Sen, Shila
Muslim politics in Bengal, 1937-1947. New Delhi. Impex India, 1976.

Sharma, P
Indian National Congress and Muslims, 1920-1940. New Delhi. Rajesh Pub., 1980.

Singhvi, L.M.
Indian political parties, New Delhi. D.K. Publishers Distributors, 1977.

Tyagi, K.G.
Foreign researches on Indian political systems & processes. Delhi. Pinka Agencies, 1984.

Yunus, Mohammad
Persons, passions and politics New Delhi. Vikas, 1980.

Zaidi, A.M.
Party politics in India V.I. pt.1. A companion volume of "Annual Register of Indian Political parties, 1987" New Delhi. D.K. Publishers & Distributors, 1980.

H b. Muslim Approaches

Abbasi. M. Yusuf
Muslim politics & leadership in South Asia, 1876-1892. Islamabad. National Institute of Historical & Cultural Research, 1981.

Ahmed, Imtiaz
Muslim political behaviour: A study of the Muslim political behaviour in Indian politics. Columbia. South Asian Book, 1978.

Ahmed, Salahuddin A.F.
Muslim Thought & leadership in Bengal in the 19th century. Essays in honour of Prof. S.C.Sarkar New Delhi. People's Pub. House, 1976.

Askari, Syed Hassan
Society and state in Islam: An introduction. New Delhi. Islam and Modern Age Soceity, 1978.

Engineer, Asghar A.
Islamic state. New Delhi. Vikas, 1980.

Goel, Sita Ram
Story of Islamic imperialism in India. New Delhi. Voice of India, 1982.

Gopal, Ram
Political history of Indian Muslims. New Delhi. Metropolitan Book Co. (Distributor), 1988.

Indian Muslims: A political history (1858-1947). Lahore. Traders, 1976.

Hardy, Peter
Partners in freedom and true Muslims. The political thought of some Muslim scholars in British India, 1912-1947. (n.p.), Student Literature, 1971.

Husain, Yusuf
Indo-Muslim polity: Turko-Afghan period. Simla. IIAS., 1971.

Khan, Qamaruddin
Al- Mawardi's theory of the State. Delhi, Idara-i-Adabiyat-i-Delli, 1979.

Political thought of Ibn. Taymiyah. New Delhi. Metropolitan Book Co., Distributor, 1988.

Khuda Bakhsh
Politics in Islam. Delhi. Idara-i-Adabiyat-i-Delhi, 1975 (rpt)

Maitra, J
Muslim Politics in Bengal, 1855-1906. Calcutta, K.P. Bagchi, 1984.

Momen, Humaira
Muslim politics in Bengal: A study of Krishak Praja Party and the election of 1937. Delhi. Sunny Home, 1972.

Nizami, Khaliq A.
Some aspects of Religion and Politics in India during the 13th Century. Delhi. Idara-i-Adabiyat-i-Delhi,1978.

State and culture in Medieval India. New Delhi. Adam, 1985.

Qureshi, I.H.
Ulema in politics: A Study Relating to the political activities of the Ulema in the South Asian subcontinent from 1556-1947. New Delhi. Renaissance Publishing House, 1985.

Shakir, Moin
Islam in Indian politics. New Delhi. Ajanta Publications, 1987.
Religion, state and politics. New Delhi. Ajanta Pub., 1987.

Zaidi, Abdul Moin,
Evolution of Muslim political thought in India. Delhi. Michiko & Panjathan 1975-1979, 6 Vols..

Muslim school of Congress; The political ideas of Muslim congress leaders from Badruddin Tayyaji to Maulana Abul Kalam Azad, 1885-1947, New Delhi. Indian bnst. Applied Political Research, 1987.

H c. Nationalism

Ahmed, Akhtaruddin
Nationalism or Islam Indo-Pakistan Episode. Delhi. D.K. Publishers, 1984.

Banergee, A.C.
Two Nations: The Philosophy of Muslim Nationalism. New Delhi. Concept Publishing, 1981.

Desai, A.R.
Social background of Indian Nationalism. Bombay. Popular Prakashan, 1970.

Hasan, Mushirul
Communal and Pan-Islamic trends in colonial India. New Delhi. Manohar Pub. 1981.

Nationalism and communal Politics in India, 1916-1928. New Delhi. Manohar Publications, 1979.

Nationalist conscience: M.A. Ansari;
The Congress and the Raj. New Delhi. Manohar, 1987.

Kaura, Uma
Muslims and Indian Nationalism: The emergence of the demand for India's; partition, 1928-1940. New Delhi, Manohar Book Service, 1977.

Pandey, B.N. ed.
The Indian nationalist movement, 1885-1947, select documents. London. Macmillan Press, 1979.

H d. Partition

Afzal, M. Rafique
Case for Pakistan. Islamabad, National Institute of Historical & Cultural Research, 1979.

Ahmad, Nuruddin
Growth of Muslim seperatism in the Indian Sub-continent, 1857-1947. London. Mansell, 1987.

Bahadur, Lal & Johari, J.C
Struggle for Pakistan in India, 1906-1947. New Delhi. Sterling, 1988.

De Amalendu
Roots of seperatism in nineteenth century Bengal. Calcutta. Patna Prakashan, 1974.

Fathipuri, F.D. Ali
Pakistan movement and Hindi-Urdu conflict. Lahore, Sang-e-Meel Publications, 1987.

Ghai, Prem V.
Partition of the Punjab, 1849-1949. New Delhi. Munshiram Manoharlal, 1986.

Hamid, Major Gen. Shahid
Disastrous twilight — A personal record of the partition of India. London. Secker and Warburg, 1986.

Hodson, H.V.
Great divide. Karachi, O.U.P., 1986.

Ikram, S.M. ed.
Modern Muslim India and the birth of Pakistan 1858-1961. Lahore. Institute of Islamic Culture, 1985

Khan, Shafique Ali
Two nations theory as a concept, strategy & ideology. Hyderabad, Markaz-e-Shaor-i-Aahbab, 1973.

Khan, Wali
Facts are facts: The untold story of India's Partition. Tr. Syeda S. Hameed. London. Sangam, 1987.

Khusro, Hamida
Separation of Sind from Bombay Presidency. v.1. Islamabad, National Institute of Historical & Cultural Research, 1982.

Kulkarni, V.B.
India & Pakistan: A historical survey of Hindu Muslim relations. Bombay. Jaico, 1973

Pakistan: Its origin and relations with India. New Delhi. Sterling, 1988.

Malhortra, S. L.
Gandhi: Punjab and the partition. Chandigarh. Publication. Bureau, 1983.

Neogy, Ajit K.
Parition of Bengal. Calcutta. A Mukherjee, 1987.

Page, David
Prelude to partition; The Indian Muslims and the imperial system of control: 1920-1932. New Delhi, O.U.P.

Philips C. H. and M.D. Wainwright Ed.
Partition of India: Policies and perspectives, 1935-1947. Bombay. Blackie, 1970.

Pirzada, S. Sharfuddin
Evolution of Pakistan. New Delhi. (Distr.: D.K. Publishers), 1988.

Robinson, Francis
Seperatism among Indian Muslims: The politics of the United Provinces Muslims, 1860-1923. New Delhi, Vikas, 1974

Rushdie, Salman
Shame. New Delhi, Rupa Paperbacks, 1983.

Shakir, Moin
Khilafat to Partition: A survey of major political trends among Indian Muslims during 1919-1947. New Delhi. Kalamkar Prakashan, 1970.

Sherwani, Latif A.
Partition of India and Mountbatten. Karachi. Council for Pakistan Studies, 1986 .

Singh, Anita I.
Origins of the Partition of India, 1936-1947. New Delhi. Oxford Univ. Press, 1987.

J. LAW

J. a. General

Ahmed, Aqil
Mohammdan Law. Allahabad. Central Law Agency, 1982.

Ali, S. Amir
Mohammdan Law, 2 v. New Delhi. Kitab Bhavan, 1986 (rpt.).

Dalvi, M.A.
Sharia: Its substance and significance. Pune. Muhammad Dalvi Waqf (pvt), 1978.

Faruqi, Kamal A.
Islamic Jurisprudence. New Delhi. Metropolitan Book Co. (Distributor), 1988.

Fyzee, A.A.A.
Outlines of Muhammadan Law. 5th Ed. David Pearl. Delhi. O.U.P., 1987.

Khuda Bakhsh Library
Catalogue of Arabic & Persian manuscripts in Khuda Bakhsh Library, Patna. v. 34. (Jurisprudence: Arabic), Patna, 1980.

Mulla, Sir Dinshah Fardunji
Principles of Muhammadan law. Bombay. N.M. Tripathi, 1977.
Principles of Muhammadan Law: with exhaustive uptodate

case law of Bangladesh, Pakistan and India. Dhaka, Dhaka law Reports, 1984.

Rahim, Sir Abdur
Principles of Muhammadan Jurisprudence according to the Hanafi, Maliki, Shafi'i and Hanbali Schools, Westport: Hyperion Press, 1981 (Rpt. of Tagore Law Lectures, 1907).

Rahman, A
Muslim Jurisprudence. Allahabad. Allahabad Law Agency, 1984

Rashid, Abdul
Muslim Jurisprudence. Allahabad. Allahabad Law Agency, 1984.

Rashid, Khalid
Muslim Law. Lucknow, Eastern Book, 1985.

Muslim Law. Lucknow, Eastern Book Co., 1970.

Tandon, Mahesh Prasad
Text-book of Mohammedan Law. Allahabad. Allahabad Law Agency, (1977).

Verma, B. Ram
Islamic law: Being a commentary on Mohammedan law. Ed. 6. Allahabad Law Pub. 1986.

Mohammedan law in India and Pakistan. Delhi Law House, 1978.

J. b. Sources

Amini, M. Taqi
Fundamentals of Ijtehad. Delhi. Idara-i-Adabiyat-i-Delhi, 1986. (IAD religious Philosophy (Original) series no. 17).

Bhatia, H.S
Studies in Islamic law, religion and society. New Delhi. Metropolitan Book Co., (Distributor), 1989.

Khadeer M. Abdul
Ijma and legislation in Islam. Secunderabad, Shivraj Press, 1974.

Khan, M Hameedullah
Schools of Islamic Jurisprudence. New Delhi. Kitab Bhavan,

Khwaja, Jamal
Authenticity and Islamic liberalism,. New Delhi. Allied, 1986.

McDonough, Sherla
Authority of the past. (American Academy of Religion: Studies in Religion). Decatur, Scholars Pr. G.A., 1976.

Merchant, M. Vallibhai
Book of Quranic Laws. New Delhi, Kitab Bhavan, 1981.

Shariff, Jaffar
Islam in India or the Qanun-i-Islam: The customs of the Musalmans of India. New Delhi. Oriental Book Corp., 1972 (rpt.)

J. c. Application/Judiciary

Ahmad, M. Basheer
Judicial system of the Mughal Empire: A study in outline of the administration of justice under the Mughal emperors based mainly on cases decided by Muslim courts in India. Karachi. Pakistan Historical Society, 1973 (Pak. Hist. Soc. Pub, 1968).

Diwan, Paras
Muslim Law in modern India. Allahabad. Law Agency, 1977.

Ewing, K. Ed.
Shariat and ambiguity in South Asian Islam. New Delhi. OUP, 1988.

Faruki, Kamal A.
Evolution of Islamic constitutional theory and practice from 610 to 1926. New Delhi. National Publishing House, 1971.

Laws and flaws. New Delhi. Metropolitan Book Co. (Distributor), 1988.

Gilani, Riaz-ul-Hasan
Reconstitution of legal thought in Islam. Delhi. Ishaat-i-Islam Trust, 1982.

Hassan, S. Riazul
Reconstrction of legal thought in Islam: A comparative study of the Islamic and the Western systems of law in the latter's terminology with particular reference to the Islamic laws suspended by the British rule in the subcontinent. Lahore. Law Pub. Co., 1974.

Husain, Wahed
Administration of Justice during the Muslim rule in India. Calcutta. Calcutta Univ. 1979, (rpt.)

Islahi, M. Yousuf
Everyday fiqh. Tr. Abdul Aziz Kamal. New Delhi. Adam Pubs., 1986.

Jain, B. S.
Administration of justice in seventeenth century India. Ed.18. Delhi. Metropolitan, 1970.

Khan, Qazi
Fatawai Qazi Khan relating to Islamic law. Tr. & ed. byMohamed Yousuf Khan Bahadur and Wilayat Husain, 2 v. New Delhi. Kitab Bhavan, 1986.

Mahmood, Tahir
Muslim Law of India, 2nd ed. Allahabad Law Book Co., 1987.

Al Marghinani, Ali Ibn Bakr
Hedaya or Guide: A commentary on the Musalman laws by Charles Hamiton, 2 v. New Delhi. Kitab Bhavan, 1986.

Markby, William
Hindu and Mohammedan Law. New Delhi. Inter-India Publications, 1977. (rpt.)

Qadri, A. A.
Justice in historical Islam. New Delhi. Kitab Bhavan, 1982.

Shad, Abdur Rehman
Do's and do nots in Islam. Delhi. Adam Pubs., 1986.

Ullah, Muhammed
Administration of Justice in Islam; An introduction to the Muslim conception of the state. New Delhi. Kitab Bhavan, 1980. (rpt.)

J. d. Succession

Ahangar, M.A.H.
Customary succession among Muslim. New Delhi. Metropolitan Book Co. (Distributor), 1986.

Bagvi, Malik B.A.
Learner's guide to the division of inheritance. New Delhi. Kitab Bhavan, 1981.

Coulson, N.J.
Succession in the Muslim family. New Delhi, Cambridge European, 1983.

Lane, Poole, S
Political & military analysis of the succession of the leadership of Muslims in India during the middle Ages. (np) Inst. Ecs. Pol., 1987

Ullah, Muhammed
Muslim law of inheritance. New Delhi, Kitab Bhavan, 1986.

J. e. Waqf

Kozlowski, Gregory C.
Muslim endowments and society in British India. Cambridage, Oxford Univ. Press, 1985.

Rahmani, R. A.
Commentaries on U.P. Muslim Waqfs Act, 1960. (U.P. act XVI of 1960), as amended up-to-date, along with bye-laws amending acts, and allied laws. Allahabad, Hind Pub. House, 1977.

J.f. Women — Legal Status

Iqbal, Safia
Women and Islamic law. New Delhi, Al.Asr Publications, 1988

Kidwai, M.H.
Women under different social and religious laws: Buddhism, Judiasm, Christianity, Islam. Delhi, Seema Pubications, 1976

Yaqin, Anwarlal & Badar Anwar
Proetection of women under the law: an annotated bibliography. New Delhi, Deep & Deep Publications, 1982.

J.g. Family Law

Ali, Zeenat S.
Marriage and Divorce in Islam: an appraisal. Bombay, Jaico, 1987.

Hussain, S. Jaffer
Marriage breakdown & divorce law reform in contemporary society: A comparative study of USA, UK & India. New Delhi, Concept, 1983.

Malik, Vijay
Muslim law of marriage, divorce and maintenance being a revised and enlarged version of A.A. Qadri's commentary on the dissolution of Marriage Act, 1939. 2nd revised ed. Lucknow, (N.P.), 1988.

Mathew, P.D. and Bakshi O.P.
Muslim marriage and divorce. New Delhi, ISI Pub., 1986.

Siddiqi, M.J.
Family laws of Islam. Delhi, Adam Pubs., 1987.

Siddiqi, Mohammed Iqbal
Family laws of Islam. New Delhi. International Islamic Pubs. 1986.

Ullah, Muhammad
Muslim law of marriage. New Delhi. Kitab Bhavan, 1986.

Verma, B.R.
Muslim marriage and dissolution. Rev. ed. Allahabad, Law Book Co., 1988.

J.h. Divorce

Ahmed, Kazi N.,
Muslim law of divorce. New Delhi, Kitab Bhavan, 1981.

Ali, Firasat and Furqan Ahmad
Divorce in Mohammdan law: The law of triple divorce. Delhi, Deep and Deep Publications, 1981.

Choudary, J.N.
Divorce in Indian society. New Delhi, Metropolitan Book Co. (Distributor), 1988.

K. ECONOMICS

K. a. Principles

Ahmed, S. Mahmud
Economics of Islam. Delhi, Idarah-i-Adabiyat, 1980.

Islahi, A. Azim
Economic concepts of Ibn Taimiyah. Leicester, Islamic Foundation, 1988.

Mannan, M. A.
Frontiers of Islamic economics. Delhi. Idarah-i-Adabiyat-i-Dilli-1985.

Islamic economic theory and practice. Delhi. Idarah-i-Adabiyat-i-Delhi, 1981.

K.b. Equality

Bhupeskhar, Ashok V. ed.
Towards socialist & transformation of Indian economy. Bombay, Popular Prakashan, 1972

K.s. Interest

Qureshi, A. Iqbal
Islam and the theory of interest. Delhi, Idarah-i-Adabiyat-i-Delhi, 1977.

Siddiqi, M. Murtzev
Recent theories of profit: critical examination. Bombay, Asia, 1971.

K.d. Money

Thorburn, S. S.
Musalamans and money lenders in the Punjab. Delhi, Mittal Publishers, 1983. (rpt.)

K.e Public Finance

Siddiqi, S. A.
Public finance in Islam. New Delhi, Adam Publications, 1982.

K.f. Social Justice

Ahmad, S Mohammad
Social justice in Islam. New Delhi, Adam Pubs., 1982.

K.g. Economic Justice

Yusuf, S. M.
Economic justice in Islam. New Delhi, Kitab Bhavan, 1988

K.h. Commerce

Arasaratnam, S.
Merchants companies and commerce on the Coromandel Coast. New Delhi, OUP., 1987.

Chaudhuri, K. N.
Trade and civilization in the Indian Ocean: an economic history from the rise of Islam to 1750. Cambridge, Oxford Univ. Press, 1985.

Chakrabarthy, Phinindrinath
Anglo-Mughal commercial relations, 1583-1717. Calcutta, OPS, 1985.

Dasgupta, A.
Indian merchants and the decline of Surat c.1700-1750. Wiesbaden: Steiner, 1979.

Indian records: commercial view of the relations between the British government and the Nawab Nazims of Bengal, Bihar & Orissa. New Delhi. D.K. Publishers Distributors, 1985. (rpt.)

Mines, M.
Muslim merchants: the economic behaviour of an Indian Muslim community. New Delhi. Shri Ram Centre for Indusrtial Relations, 1972.

Pant, D.
Commercial policy of the Mogals. Delhi, Idarah-i-Adabiyat-i-Delhi, 1978.

Pearson, M.N.
Merchants and rulers in Gujrat: The response to the Portuguese in the sixteenth century. Berkeley, U. California Press, 1976.

Sarkar, H. B.
Trade & commercial activities of Southern India in Malaya-Indonesian world. Calcutta, Firma K L M, 1987

Singh, O.P.
Surat and its trade in the second half of the 17th Century. Delhi: Universituy of Delhi, 1977.

L. EDUCATION AND LEARNING

L. a. Traditional

Adam, W.
One teacher, one school, the Adam reports on indigenous education in 19th century India. Ed. Dibona, J. Delhi: Biblia Impex, 1983.

Ahmad, M. Akhlaq
Traditional education among Muslims: a study of some aspects in modern India. Delhi, B.R. Pub., 1985.

Ahmad, M. Ashfaque
Systems of education in medieval India: 1526-1761 A.D. New Delhi, Panchsheel, 1987.

Chopra, Pran Nath
Life and letters under the Mughals. New Delhi. Ashajanak Pubications, 1976.

Desai, Ziyauddin
Centres of Islamic learning in India. Delhi. Publications Division, Ministry of Information and Broadcasting, 1978.

Dharmpal
The beautiful tree: indigenous Indian education in the eighteenth century. Delhi. Biblia Impex. 1983. 343pp.

Jaffar, S M
Education in Muslim India. Delhi. Idarah-i-Adabiyat-i-Delhi, 1973. (rpt.)

Khan, M. S.
Islamic education. New Delhi, Ashish, 1985.

Metcalf, Barbara D
Islamic revival in British India: Deoband, 1860-1900. New Jersey, Princeton Univ. Press, 1982.

Quraishi, M. A.
Some aspects of Muslim education. Baroda, Baroda Univ. Pub., 1970.

Quraishi, Mansur-ud-din
Muslim education and learning in Gujarat, 1297-1758. Baroda, M.S. Univ., 1972.

Rahman, Mohibur
History of madrasah education (with special reference to Calcutta Madrasah and West Bengal Madrasah Board). Calcutta, Rais Anwar Rahman & Bros., 1977.

Ray, K. Lal
Education in Medieval India. Delhi. B.R. Pub. Corporation, 1984.

Troll, Christian W.
Islam in India: Studies and commentaries v.g: Religion and religious education. New Delhi. Vikas, 1985.

I.b. Modern

Basu, Aparna
Growth of education and political development in India. Delhi (np), 1974.

Hari, Om
Muslims of Jammu: A study in the spread of education and consciousness 1857-1925. New Delhi, Archives Publication, 1986.

Hashmi, Masroor
Muslim response to western education. New Delhi, Gian (Distributor for Commonwealth Publisher), 1987.

Kirmani, M. Zaki
Western civilization: Impact on individual, society and knowledge. Aligarh, Nai Naslen Pub., 1983.

Mathew, A.
Christian missions, education & nationalism: From dominance to compromise, 1870-1930. New Delhi, Anamika Prakashan, 1988.

Mohammed, Y. Sayed
What is Islamization of knowledge? Tirunelveli, Muhammad Taahaa Pub., 1988.

Moin, Mumtaz
The Aligarh movement (Origin and early history). Karachi:. Salman Academy, 1976.

Muhammad, Shan Ed.
Aligarh movement: Basic document, 1864-1898. 3 v. Meerut, Meenakshi, 1978.

Muttalib, M. A.
Voluntary action in education. Delhi, Sterling, 1989.

Shah, Shamim
Educational survey report on Muslim managed schools and colleges in India with special emphasis on science education. New Delhi, Hamdard Education Soc., 1985.

Sharma, Krishan Dev
Education of a national minority: A case of Indian Muslim. Kalamkar, Prakashan, 1978.

Siddiqui, M.K.A.
Educating a backward minority. Calcutta, Abadi Pub., 1985.

Singh, Mohinder Comp.
Learned societies and institutions in India, activities and publications: Including over 4,000 research oriented titles. Delhi, Metropolitan Book, 1975,

Tonki, S.M
Aligarh & Jamia fight for national education system. New Delhi. People's Pub. House, 1983.

L. c. Language
L. c. a. General

Razi, F D
Modern Persian Dictionary (Persian-Urdu-English) New Delhi, Kitab Bhavan, 1981.

Sabri, M. and Ghariat A.B.
English-Urdu-Pushto-Persian coversation. Lahore. Malik Book, Depot. 1986.

L. c. b. Arabic

Agaskar, Yunus
Arabic for everybody's use. Bombay, Jaico, 1984.

Ali, S. Abbas
Arabic for Beginners. Madras, Arabic Pub. of India, 1970.

Howell, Mortimer S.
Grammar of the classical Arabic language. New Delhi, Gian, 1986.

Khan, M.A. Saleem
Arabic for scholars of social science. Delhi, Darud Alm. 1982.

Steingass, F.
Learner's Arabic-English dictionary. New Delhi, Sterling, 1986.

Learner's English-Arabic dictionary, New Delhi, sterlins, 1986

L. c. c. Persian

Jones Sir William
Garmmar of the Persian language. Delhi, (Dist.: D.K. Publishers), 1982.

L. c. d. Sanskrit

Chaudhuri, J. Bimal

Muslim patronage to Sanskritic learning v. I. Delhi. Idarah-i-Adabiyat-i-Delhi, 1981.

L. c. e. Urdu

Ahmad, Mumtaz
Urdu Newspaper Reader. Dunwoody Pr., 1985

Barker, Muhammad.
Spoken Urdu. (Spoken Language Ser.) Spoken Language Service, 1975.

Barker, Muhammad & Hamdani.
Urdu, Vol. I Norton Pubs., 1975.
Urdu, Vol.II. J Norton Pubs., 1976

Barker, Muhammad Abd-al-Rahman, et al.
Urdu Newspaper Reader. (Spoken Language Ser). Spoken Lang Serv., 1974

Becker, Donald.
Reverse dictionary of Urdu. Manohar, (Urdu.). 1980
s
Bender, Ernest.
Urdu: Grammar & reader. Bks Demand UMI., 1980.

Bright, William & Khan, Saeed A.
The Urdu writing system. Spoken Lang Serv., 1976

Chandoia, Anoop
A Systematic translation of Hindi-Urdu into English. U of Ariz Pr., 1970.

Dewan, Parvez.
Hindi-Urdu phasebook. Lonely Planet. 1988.

Dhillion, Harinder J
Thirty two basic steps into Urdu vocabulary. A Vocabulary Workbook. (Illus). H J Dhillon., 1986.

Diehl, Katharine S.
Persian, Arabic, & Urdu printing in Bengal, from 1778. (Printers & Printing in the East Indies to 1850 Set: Vol V). Caratzas. 1988.

The Press Beyond Calcutta-North & East (Printers & Printing in the East Indies to 1850 Set: Vol. VI). Caratzas. 1989.

Ferozsons Urdu Encyclopaedia: Pictorial, 4 Color, Kazi Pubns. 1980.

Ferozsons, ed. Urdu-English-English-Urdu Dictionary, 2 vols. rev & enl.ed. Ibd Ltd., 1986.

Learn Urdu for English Speakers. Saphrograph. 1986.

Pakistani. English-Urdu Dictionary. (Eng & Urdu.). Kazi Pubns., 1985.

Haq, Abdul
Practicial advanced twentieth century dictionary: English into English and Urdu. Comp. by Bashir Ahmed Qureshi. New Delhi. Anjum Book Depot, 1989. Student edition.

Practical standard twentieth century dictionary: Urdu into English. Comp. by Bashir Ahmed Qureshi New Delhi, Anjum Book Depot, 1988. Student Edition.

Standard English-Urdu Dictionary. Delhi. J.S. Sant Singh and Sons, 1975.

Sangaji, S.
Urdu-English Dictionary. (Urdu & Eng.). French & Eur., 1983.

Urdu-English Dictionary, Romanized. (Urdu & Eng.), Saphrograph, 1988.

Urdu Newspaper Articles, Romanized (Urdu & Eng.). Saphrograph., 1985.

Urdu Newspaper Articles (For Reading Comprehension) H.J. Dhillon., 1987

L d. Literature
L d a. General

Ayyub, A. Sayeed
Poetry and truth: a philosophical essay on modern poetry. Calcutta, Jadavpur, Univ., 1970.

Dalvi, M.A.
Islamic tales (Moral). Pune. Muhammad Dalvi Waqf (Pvt.) 1985.

Dictionary of Oriental Literatures. 3 v. Delhi. Vikas, 1975.

Encyclopaedia of Indian Literature. 4 v. New Delhi. Sahitya Akademi, 1975.

George, K.M.ed.
Comparative Indian Literature. Trivandrum. Kerala Sahitya Akademi, 1983.

Ghalib, Mirza
Candle's smoke. Tr. Inderjet lal. Delhi. Saluja Prakashan, 1970.

Dastanbuy: A Diary of the Indian Revolt of 1857. Tr. K.A. Faruqui. Bombay. Asia, 1970.

Twenty-Five Verses. Tr. C.M. Naim. Calcutta. Writers Workshop, 1970.

Hansen, W
Peacock Throne: The drama of Mogul India. New Delhi. Motilal Banarsidass, 1971.

Hasule, A
Novels of Khwaja Ahmad Abbas. New Delhi. Metropolitan Book, Co. (Distributors), 1987.

Howarth, S.
Koh-i-noor diamond: the history and the lenged. London: Quartet Book, 1980.

Hosain, Attia
Sunlight on a broken column. New Delhi, Arnold Heinemann, 1979. (rpt.)

Hyder, Qurratulain
Women's Life. New Delhi, Chetna, 1979.

Indian council for cultural Relations, New Delhi.
Indian Literature; Select biblographies, ed. H.S. Patil and Saiyyad Masih ul Hasan New Delhi. Vikas, 1972. (Aspects of Indian Culture, B).

Iqbal, Sir Muhammad
Armaghan-i-Hijaz: versified English translation, by Q. A. Kabir. Lahore, Iqbal Academy, 1984.

Islam as an ethical and a political ideal. (Iqbal's maiden English lecture, 1980); ed. with a critical introduction ... by S.Y. Hashmy. 2 nd rev. ed. Lahore: Islamic Book Service, 1977.

Longer poems of Iqbal. Done into English by A.R. Tariq. Lahore. Ghulam Ali & Sons, 1978.

The poet's vision and magic of words an approach to Iqbal's poetry. Lahore. Islamic Book Service, 1971.

Islam, Kabirul.
The home-coming. Translated from Bengali by Ketaki Kushari Dyson. Calcutta. Writers Workshop, 1982. (Poems)

Jain, C.R.
Gems of Islam: Lifting of the veil. pt. 1. New Delhi. Today & Tomorrow, 1975.

Karnad, Girish Raghunath
Tuglaq. New Delhi, OUP., 1972.

Kaul, H. L, ed.
Historic Delhi: An Anthology. New Delhi. OUP. 1985.

Kritzeck, James ed.
Anthology of Islamic literature.: From rise of Islam to modern times New York. New Am. Lib., 1975.

Manto, Saadat Hasan
Kingdom's end and other stories. London. Verso, 1987.

Best of Manto: A collection of his short stories edited and translated by Jai Ratan. New Delhi, Sterling, 1989.

Metcalf, Barbara D. ed.
Moral conduct and authority: The place of adab in South Asian Islam. Berkeley, Univ. of California Press, 1984.

Metcalf, Thomas ed.
Modern India: An interpretative anthology. London. Collier-Macmillan, 1971.

Mishra, Udayon
Ray in fiction. A study of nineteenth century British attitudes towards India. Delhi. B.R. Pub. Corp., 1987.

Nadvi, Abul Hassan A.
Tales of the Prophet. Pt.1 Lucknow, Academy of Islamic Research, 1976.

Parvez, Salahuddin
Namrita. (Translated from the Urdu by the author.) Aligarh: SL. 1984.

Raja, P
Tales of Mulla Nasiruddin. New Delhi. (Distr.: D.K. Publishers), 1988.

Rizvi, Iftikkar Husain
Thirty pebbles and other poems. Bareilly, Prakash Book Depot, 1987.

Ruswa, Mirza Mohammad Hadi
Courtesan of Lucknow. Tr. from Urdu by Khushwant Singh and M.A. Husaini. Delhi. Hind Pocket Books, 1970.

Salim, M. Kunju
Golden stories. New Delhi. Kitab Bhavan, 1985.

Samarrai, Qasim al.
How a western scholar interprets Islamic prophetic tales (A review article of a mystical interpretation of prophetic tales by an Indian Muslim. Shah Wali Allah's Ta'Wil al-Ahadit by J.M.S. Baljon) Leiden. New Rhine Publishers, 1970.

Sanker, Brijendra Mohan, Ed.
India: A nineteenth century study of British imperialism in verse. New Delhi, Kumar Bros, 1972.

Sen, S.P., ed.
Historical biography in Indian literature. Calcutta. Calcutta Institute of Historical Studies, 1979.

Schimmel, Annemarie
Islamic literatures of India (History of Indian Literature series. v. 7.) Fasc.1 Part.1) Wiesbaden, Otto Harrasowitz, 1973.

Shah, Amina V.
The tale of the four dervishes of Amir Khusru retold. London: Octagon Press, 1976.

Sharma, K.K. and B.K. Johri
Partition in Indian English novels. Ghaziabad, Vimal Prakashan, 1984.

Sharma, Nasira, ed.
Echoes of revolution: Poems of revolt and liberation. Transaltions in Hindi, Urdu and English with originals in Persian. New Delhi, Vikas, 1979.

Shawq, Nawab Mirza
Zahr-i-ishq or Poison of love (a love narrative from Awadh) Tr. Abdus Salam. Shah & Donaghue.J., Delhi, D.K. 1983. (Urdu text with facing English translation & glossory).

Siddiqi, Iqtidar H.
Modern writings on Islam & Muslims in India. Aligarh, International Book Traders, 1974.

Singh, Khushwant and Qurratulain Hyder, ed.
Stories from India, New Delhi, Sterling, 1974.

Singh, Shailandra
Novels on the Indian Mutiny. New Delhi, Arnold Heinemann, 1973

Skyhawk, High Van, ed.
Minorities on themselves (South Asian Digest of Regional Writing, v. 2). Stuttgart, Steiner Verlag, 1986.

South Asian Digest of Regional Writing. v. 5. Heidelberg, South Asian Institute, University of Heidelberg, 1979.

Stein, Aurel
Hatim's Tales. New Delhi, Gian, 1988.

Who's who of Indian Writers, 1983, New Delhi, Sahitya Akademy, 1983.

Yunus Mohammad
Letters from Prison. New Delhi, Vikas, 1987.

Zbavitel, Dusan, ed.
Dictionary of Oriental literatures v 2. South and South-East Asia. New York. Basic Books, 1974.

L. d. b. Arabic

Ashraf, Muhammad
A concise descriptive catalogue of the Arabic Manuscripts in the Salar Jung Museum & Library. Volume IV: concerning 448 manuscripts of Islamic theology (Shiite) Hyderabad. Salar Jung Museum & Library, 1981 (Salar Jung Museum & Library Publication, New Series: 10/4).

Asiatic Society, Calcutta
Catalogue of Arabic manuscripts in tabular form. Prepared by K.M. Mitra. Rev. and ed. by M.S. Khan. Calcutta, 1980.

Fariq, K.A.
History of Arabic literature. Delhi. Vikas, 1972.

Hai, M.A.
Quranic stories. Delhi. Maktaba Achasnat, 1984.

L. d.c Bengali

Ashraf, Syed Ali
Muslim traditions in Bengali literature. 3rd ed. Dhaka. Islamic Foundation, 1983.

L. d. d. Persian

Abidi, S.A. Hasan
India's rich and valuable contribution to Persian literature in the light of some recent discoveries. Patna: Khuda Baksh Oriental Public Library, 1982 (Khuda Baksh Annual Lecture:9)

Ghalib, Mirza
Persian ghazals of Ghalib. Tr. Yusuf Husain. New Delhi. Ghalib Academy, 1980.

Hillmann, Michael C.
Twentieth century Persian literature in translation; a bibliography Washington, Cultural Department, Imperial Embassy of Iran, 1976.

Khuda Baksh Oriental Public Library
Catalogue of Arabic & Persian manuscripts in Khuda Baksh Library, Patna, v3. (Persian Poetry) Patna, 1977.

Catalogue of Arabic & Persian manuscripts in Khuda Baksh Library. Patna, v.31 (Poetry alongwith history, biography, Tales & Anthology: Persian).

Rahman, A.C.
Persian literature in India during the time of Jahangir and Shahjahan. Baroda. M.S. University, 1970.

Yohannan, John D.
Persian poetry in England and America: a 200-year history. Delmar, N.Y. Caravan Books, 1977. (Persian studies series).

L. d. e. Urdu

Ali, Ahmed
The golden tradition: an anthology of Urdu poetry. New York, Columbia Univ. Press, 1973

Baidar, Bakht and K.G. Jaeger
Anthology of modern Urdu poetry, v.1. Delhi, Educational Pub. House, 1983.

Baig, Farhatullah
Last mushairah of Delhi. Tr. Akhter Qamer. New Delhi, Orient Longman, 1979.

Barker, Muhammad A
A Reader of Classical Urdu Poetry, 3 vols. Spoken Lang Serv. 1977.

Ghalib, Mirza
Urdu ghazels of Ghalib. Tr. Yousuf Husain Delhi, Ghalib Academy, 1979.

Urdu letters of Mirza Asadullah Khan Ghalib. Tr. Daud Rahbar. New York, State University of New York, 1987.

Kaul, H.K.
Urdu manuscripts: A descriptive bibliography of manuscripts in Delhi libraries. New Delhi, Heritage Publishers. 1977.

Kesavan, B.S. ed.
National bibliography of Indian literature, 1901-1953 Vol II: Sindhi, Tamil, Telugu, Urdu. New Delhi, Shitya Academy, 1974.

Mirza, Agha Iqbal
Modern Urdu stories. Calcutta: Writers workshop, 1975.

Narang, Gopi C.
Urdu: Readings in literary Urdu prose. Ann Arbor, Bks Demand UMI, 1970.

Pritchett, Francis W.
Urdu literature: A bibliography of English language sources. New Delhi, Manohar, 1979.

Rai, Amrit.
A House Divided: The origin & development of Hindi-Hindavi. Oxford U Pr. 1985.

Ratan, Jai
Modern Urdu short stories: Selected and translated. New Delhi, Allied, 1987.

Sadiq, Muhammad
History of Urdu literature. 2nd ed. New York, Oxford Univ. Press, 1984.

Schimmel, Annamarie
Classical Urdu literature: From the beginning to Iqbal (History of Indian Literature Series. v.8. Fase.3) pt.1) Weisbadin, Otto Hurrasowitz, 1975.

Siddiqi, M. Atiq
Origins of modern Hidustani literature. (Source Materials: Gilchirst letters) New Delhi, Kitab Bhavan, 1979.

Zaidi, Ali J.
Mir Anis, Urdu poet. New Delhi, Sahtya Academy, 1986.

Zia, Abdul Q.
Urdu poetry in contemporary setting: A study in historical perspectives. Hongkong, Asian Research Service, 1989.

M. HISTORY

M. a. Historiography

Ali, B. Sheikh
History: Its theory and method. 2nd ed. Madras, Macmillan, 1978.

Ali, Hashim Amir
Reconstruction of Islamic chronology. Patna, Khuda Baksh Oriental Pub. Lib., 1980.

Askari, Syed H.
Maktub amd Malfuz literature as a source of socio-political history. Patna, Khuda Baksh Oriental Public Library, 1981.

Devahuti,
Bias in Indian historiography. New Delhi. D.K. Publishers, 1980.

Sarkar, Jagdish Narayan.
History of history—writing in Medieval India: Contemporary historians. An introduction to medieval Indian historiography. Calcutta: Ratna Prakashan, 1977.

Romance of historiography from Shah Alam I to Shah Alam II (non-European). Calcutta. Ratna Prakashan, 1982.

Syed, M. Aslam
Study of Muslim historiography in India from 1857-1914. Islamabad, National Institute of Historical & Cultural Research, 1989.

M. b. Sources

Ahmad, Riaz.
Iqbal's letters to Quaid-i-Azam: An analysis. Lahore. Friends Educational Service, 1976.

American Institute of Indian Studies
Primary sources for 16th-19th century studies in Bengal, Orissa and Bihar libraries Ed. Katharine S. Diehl. Calcutta, 1971.

Andhra Pradesh, State Archives:
A descriptive catalogue of the documents pertaining to the reign of Shah Jahan, 1628-1658. V.1 Hyderabad, 1977.

Mughal documents: Catalogue of Auranzeb's reign. Ed. and comp. by M.A. Nayeem. V.1 Pt. 1. Hyderabad, 1980.

Ansari, Mukhtar Ahmed
Muslims and the Congress; Select correspondence of Dr. M A. Ansari, 1912-35. Edited by Mushirul Hasan New Delhi, Manohar, 1979.

Badayuni, Abdul Qadir
Muntakhab-ut-Twarikh v.1 Tr. by S.A. Ranking Patna, Academica Associated, 1973.

Muntakhab-ut-Twarikh v.2 Tr. W.H. House Patna, Academica Asiatica, 1973.

Muntakhab-at-Twarikh v.3. Tr. Wolsely Haig. Patna. Academica Asiatica, 1973.

Bendrey, V. S.
Study of Muslim inscriptions, with special reference to the inscriptions, published in the Epigraphia Indo-Moslemica, 1907-1938. Delhi, Anmol Publications, 1985.

Bernier, Francois
Travels in the Mogul empire: AD 1656-1668. New Delhi, Munshiram Manoharlal, 1983

Bilmoria, J. H
Letters of Aurangzeb. Delhi. Idara-i-Adabiyat-i-Delhi 1973.

Biruni, al-
Albiruni's India. Abriged Edition of Edward Sachau's Translation. Ed. Qeyamaddin Ahmed. New Delhi, NBT, 1981.

Alberuni's India, Edited by E.C. Sachau. 2v (bound in one). New Delhi, Munshiram Manoharlal, 1983

Desai, Ziyauddin
Published Muslim inscriptions of Rajasthan. Jaipure, Directorate of Archaeology & Museums, 1971.

Dunn, R.E.
Adventures of Ibn Batuta. London, Crom Helm, 1986.

Datta, V.N. and Cleghorn, B.E.
A nationalist Muslim and Indian politics: Being the selected correspondence of Late Dr. Syed Mahmud. Delhi, Macmillan, 1974.

Elliot, Henry M.
Mohammadan period as described by its own Historians. Selected from the works of Sir Henry M Elliot. New Delhi, Asian Educational Services, 1986.

Mohammadan Period as described by its own Historian. v.5. New Delhi, Asian Educational Service, 1987.

Firdausi
Shah namah. Tr. by Alexander Rogers. New Delhi, Heritage, 1978.

Firishtah, Muhammad
History of the rise of the Mohamadan power in India until 1612. 4 vols. Tr. by John Higgs. Calcutta, Mukhopadhya, 1971.

Gibb, A. R.
Ibn Battuta: Travels in Asia and Africa. New York, State Mutual Book, 1983.

Grewal, J. S.
Medieval Indian history and historicals. Amritsar, Guru Nanak Dev. Univ., 1975.

Muslim rule in India; the assessments British historians, Bombay, OUP 1970.

Henderson, J. R.
Coin of Haidar Ali & Tipu Sultan Delhi, D.K. Publishers Distributors, 1987 (rpt)

Husaini, K. K.
Maasir-e-Jahangir: A contemporary account of Jahangir. Edited by Azra Alavi. Bombay, Asia, 1978.

Iqbal, Sir Muhammad.
Letters of Iqbal, ed. by Bashir Ahamd Dar. Lahore: Iqbal Academy Pakistan, 1978.

Isami, Abd al-Malik,
Futuhu's-salatin or Shah namah-i-Hind: Translation and commentary, ed. by Mahdi Husain, Vols. 2 and 3. New York: Asia Publishing House, 1976-77.

Jahangir, Nuruddin Muhammad
Autobiographical memories of Emperor Jahangir. Calcutta, Editions Indian, 1972.

Jouher,
Tezkhereh-a Vakiat or private memories of the Moghul Emperor Humayun. Tr. Charles Stewart. Lucknow, Pustak, 1974

Kausar, Kabir
Secret correspondence of Tipu Sultan. New Delhi, Light & Life Publishers, 1980 (rpt)

Khan, Muhammad Hadi Kamwar
Tazkirat salatin Chagtai: a Mughal chronicle of post Aurangzeb period, 1707-1724; Persian text edited with notes and introduction by Muzaffar Alam. Bombay. Asia Publishing House, 1980.

Khan, M.A. Wali
Copper coins of Adil Shahi Dynasty of Bijapur. Hyderabad. Birla Archaeological & Cultural Research Institute, 1980.

Khan, Mirza, Abu Talib
Travels of Mirza Abu Taleb Khan in Asia, Africa and Europe during the year 1799 to 1803. Tr. from Persian by Charles Stewart. New Delhi, Sona Pub., 1972.

Khan, Shafaat A.
Sources for the study of British India in the 17th century. Delhi. Pankaj Publications, 1986.

Khan S. Ali
History and historians of Rajasthan. Delhi, Triveni, 1981.

Khani, Mohammed Bihammed
Tarikh-i-Muhammadi. Tr. Muhammad Zaki. Bombay, Asia, 1972.

Khusraw, Amir.
India, as seen by Amir Khusraw (in 1318 A D) Tr. R. Nath & Faiyaz Gwahliari. Jaipur, Historical Research Documentation

Programme. 1981 (Translation of the third chapter of Nuh Siphir also known at the Sultan-nama)

Lane-Poole, Stanley
Coins and medals; their place in history and art. New Delhi, Cosmo, 1982.

Coins of the Moghul Emperors of Hindustan in the British Museum. New Delhi, Inter India Pub., 1983.

Marshall, D N.
The Afghans in India under the Delhi Sultanate and the Mughal Empire: a survey of relevant manuscripts. Ed. by C.J. Brunner New York: The Asia Society, 1976 (Afghanistan Council, Occasional papers, 10)

History of Libraries: Ancient and Medieval. New Delhi, Oxford and I.B.H., 1984.

Martin, Francois
Memories of India in the 17th Century, 1670-1694 Memoirs. Tr. by Lotika Vardaraja. v. 1. New Delhi, Manohar, 1981.

Minhajaddin, Mubarak
Tabakat-i-Nasiri, a general history of the Mohammadan Dynasties of Asia including Hindustan, 2 V. Tr. by H. G. Raverty. New Delhi, Munshiram Manoharlal, 1970.

Mohiuddin, Momin
Chancellery and Persian epistolography under the Mughals, from Babar to Shahjahan, 1526-1658: A study on Insha, Dar al Insha, and Munshi. Based on original documents. Calcutta, Iran Society, 1971.

Mohammad, Shan. ed.
Unpublished letters of the Ali Brothers. Delhi, Idarah-i-Adabiyat-i-Delhi, 1984

Mukhia, Harbans
Historians and historiography during the reign of Akbar. New Delhi, Vikas, 1976.

Nizami, Ganjawi
Sikandar Nama or Book of Alexander the Great. Written in A.D. 1200 by Abu Mohammad bin Yusuf bin Muayyid-i- Nizamuddin. Tr. Wilberforce Clarke. New Delhi, Vikas, 1979.

Nizami, Khaliq A.
On history and historians of medieval India. New Delhi, Munshiram Manoharlal, 1983.

O'connor, V.C. Scott
An Eastern Library: An introduction to Khuda Bakshsh Library. Patna, Khuda Baksh Oriental Public Library, 1977.

Parihar, Subhesh
Muslim inscriptions in the Punjab, Haryana and Himachal Pradesh. New Delhi, D.K. Publishers, Distributors, 1985.

Rodgers, C.J.
Catalogue of the coins: The coins of the Mughal Emperors of India, 4 vols. New Delhi. D.K. Publishers, Distributors, 1985. (rpt.)

Sarkar, Jadunath
History of Aurangzeb based on Original sources. 5 v. New Delhi, Orient Longman, 1974.

Seddon, C. N. and Syed Nawab Ali Tr
Mirat-i-Ahmadi Supplement. Baroda, Oriental Inst., 1982.

Sirhindi, Yahiya Bin Ahmad Bin Abdullah
Tarikh-i-Mubarakshahi, Tr. into English from the Persian by T.T. Beveridge. Delhi, MLBD, 1986.

Tirmizi, S.A.I
Mughal documents, 1526-1627. New Delhi, Gian, 1989.

Umari, Shihabul Din
Fourteenth century Arab account of India under Sultan Muhammad Bin Tughluq. Tr. I. H. Siddiqi & Q.M. Ahmad. Aligarh, Siddique Pub. House, 1972.

Viquar, S. Nasiruddin
5000 years Gregorian Calendar with comparative table of Hegiri & Gregorian tables. Hyderabad, Imam-ul-uloom Education Society, 1983.

Wheeler, J. Talboys, ed.
Early travels in India (16th & 17th Centuries). Delhi, Deep and Deep pub., 1975.

Williams, L. F. Rushrook
Ayeen-i-Akbari. Delhi, Idarah-i-Adabiyat-i-Delhi, 1975.

Wright, H. Nelson
Coins of the Mughal emperors of India. Delhi, Deep and Deep Pub., 1975.

Ojha, V.S. Gaurishanker
Cropus inscription Bhavanagar: Being a selections of Arabic & Persian inscriptions collected by Antiquarian Department, Bhavanagar State. New Delhi, Kumar Bros, 1971.

Zaki, Muhammad
Arab Accounts of India During the Fourteenth Century. Delhi, Idarah-i-Adabiyat-i-Delhi, 1981.

M. C. India: General

Abidi, Sartaj A. and Sharma, S.K.
Fifty years of Indian history writings. Index Articles in Journal of Indian History. v.1-50 (1921/22 1972), New Delhi, Gitanjali Prakashan, 1974

Allen, N.J. et al
Oxford University Papers on India. V.1 Pt.1 New Delhi, OUP, 1987.

Asiatic Society, Calcutta
Asiatic researches, comprising history and anti- quities, the arts, science and literature of Asia, 24 v. New Delhi, Cosmo, 1979.

Bajpai, S. C.
Northern frontier of India. Bombay, Allied, 1970.

Banerjee, Anil
Aspects of Rajput states and society. New Delhi, Rajesh Pub., 1983.

Barnett, Richard, B.
North India Between Empires Awadh, the Mughals and the British: 1720-1801. New Delhi, Metropolitan Book Co., (Distributor) 1987.

Bhattacherje, S. B.
Encyclopaedia of Indian dates & events. New Delhi, Sterling, 1987.

Chaudhuri, Radhakrishna
History of Muslim rule in Tirhut, 1206-1765 A D. Varanasi, Chowkhamba, 1970.

Chopra, Usha
Medieval and modern India. New Delhi. Sultan Chand, 1983.

Crooke, William
North-Western provinces of India; their history, ethnology and administration. Delhi, Indological, 1971.

Dogra, R.C.
Catalogue of the early printed books on South Asia: From 1586 to 1864 held in the library of School of Oriental and African Studies, London. New Delhi, Aditya Prakashan, 1988.

Donovan, W. and P.E. Daniel
Essays in Indian History, New Delhi, Asia Pub., 1973.

Elliott, Henry M and John Dawson
Supplimentary History of India V.2-3Ed. Khaliq A. Nizami. Delhi, Idarah-i-Adabiyat-i-Delhi, 1981.

Faqih, Irfan
Glimpses of Indian History. New Delhi, D.K. Publishers, Distributors, 1988.

Guiaud, J
Ruins of Mandoo, the ancient Mahommeden capital of Malwah, in Central India: From the original sketches of Captain Claudius Harris. Ahmedabad, New Order Book Co., 1985.

Gurney, Gene
Kingdoms of Asia, The Middle East and Africa: An illustrated encyclopaedia of ruling monarchs from ancient times to the present. New York, Crown, 1986.

Ishwari Prasad
Short history of Muslim rule in India from the advent of Islam to the death of Aurangzeb. Allahabad, Indian Press, 1970.

Jackson, A.V. Williams ed.
From the sixth century B.C. to the Mohammedan conquest including the Invasion of Alexander the Great. v.2. New Delhi, AES, 1987.

Keene, Henry G.
Sketch of the History of Hindustan from the first Muslim conquest to the fall of Mughal Empire Delhi, Idarah-i-Adabiyat-i-Delhi, 1972.

Khan, Ghulam Hussain
History of Mohammadan power in India. Tr John Briggs. Delhi, Idarah-i-Adabiyat-i-Delhi, 1973.

Khuda Bakhsh Library
Catalogue of Arabic & Persian manuscripts in Khuda Baksh Library, Patna v.7 (Indian history: Persian) Patna, 1977

Kulke, H and D. Rothermund
History of India. London, Routledge, 1986.

Mahajan, V.D.
Mohommedan dynasties. New Delhi, Lotus Pub., 1986.

Muslim rule in India. New Delhi, S. Chand, 1984.

Price, David
Mohommedan history: From the death of the Arabian le- gislator to the accession of the emperor Akbar and the establishment of the Moghul empire in Hindustan. 3V in 4 Pts. New Delhi, II P, 1984

Rees, John David,
The Muslim epoch. ed.2. New Delhi, Asian Publication Service, 1980.

Sewell, R
Indian before the English. New Delhi, Asian Educational Service, 1986.

Somani, Ram Vallath.
History of Mewar (from earliest times to 1751 A.D.) Jaipur: C.L. Ranka & Co. 1976 (includes Sultan Alauddin)

Saeed, Mian Muhammad
Sharqi Sultanate of Jaunpur. Jaipur, Historical Research Documentation Programme Distributor, 1972.

Tirmizi, S.A.I.
Indian historical vistas. New Delhi, Munshiram Manoharlal, 1980.

Wheelers, W. J
India under the Muslim rule. New Delhi, Cosmo, 1975.

M. d. Sultanate Period (Medieval):
M. d. a. General

Aligarh Muslim University (Aligarh)
Medieval India: A miscellany. v.2. Bombay, Asia, 1972.

Banerjee, Anil C.
New history of medieval India. New Delhi. S. chand, 1986.

Day, Upendra N.
Some aspects of medieval Indian history. New Delhi, Rajesh Pub., 1982.

Hamadani, Agha Hussain
Frontier policy of the Delhi Sultans. Islamabad: National Institute of Historical and Cultural Research, 1986.

Ishwari Prasad
History of medieval India. Allahabad, Indian Press, 1970.

Joshi, Rakha
Facets of Delhi Sultanate. Allahabad. Kitab Mahal, 1976.

Lal, Vinod Behari
Medieval India, 711 AD 103 AD. Lucknow, Prakashan Kendra, 1971.

Lane-Poole, Stanley
Medieval India under Mohammedan rule (A D 712-1764). Delhi. Universal Books and Stationery Co., 1970.

The Mohammadan dynasties: Chronological and geneological tables with historical introductions. Delhi, Idarah-i Adabiyat-i Delhi, 1977.

Lauwani, K. C.
Medieval muddle. Calcutta. 'Prajnanam, 1982.

Mahajan, V. D.
Delhi Sultanate. Ed 4. New Delhi, S. Chand, 1970.

History of medieval India. New Delhi, S. Chand, 1986.

Sultanate of Delhi (712 AD to 1526 AD). Ed 6. New Delhi, S. Chand, 1984.

Mazumdar, Sukumar
Medieval India: A miscellany. Ed. by K. A. Nizami. Bombay, Asia, 1975.

Mehta, J. L.
Advanced study in the history of medieval India. 3v. New Delhi, Sterling, 1983.

Misra, R. G.
Indian resistance to early Muslim invaders up to 1206 A.D. Meerut, Anu. 1983.

Nizami, Khaliq A. and Mohammad Habib
Comprehensive History of India. V.5. A.D. 1206 - 1526: The Delhi Sultanate. New Delhi, People's Publishing House, 1987.

Owen, Sidney J.
From Mahmud Ghazni to the disintegration of Mughal Empire. Delhi, Kanishka, 1987.

Rizvi, S.A. Abbas
The wonder that was India, V.2.: 1200-1700 (Sidgwick and Jackson Great Civilization Series). London, Sidgwick and Jackson, 1987.

Sharma, L. P.
History of medieval India, (1000 A.D.-1740 A.D). New Delhi, Konark, 1987.

Medieval history of India. New Delhi, Vikas, 1981.

Sultanate of Delhi. New Delhi, Konark, 1987.

Sharma S.L.
Sultanate of Delhi 711-1526 AD. Agra, Shiv Lal Agarwal, 1981.

Sharma, S. R.
Crescent in India: A study in medieval history. Delhi, Sanjay Prakashan, 1985.

Singh, Meera
Medieval history of India. New Delhi, Vikas, 1977.

Sullivan, Edward.
Conquerers, warriors, statesmen of India: A historical narrative of the principal events from the invasion of Mahmud of Ghazni to that of Nadir Shah. Delhi, Motilal Banarsidass, 1985.

Thapar, Romila
Medieval India. Delhi, Ind - Us Inc., 1970.

Tirmizi, S.A.I.
Miscellany of medieval India. New Delhi, International Writers, 1986.

Vaidya, C.V.
Downfall of Hindu India. New Delhi, Gian, 1986.

M. d. a. Ghaznavids

Jaffar, S. M.
Medieval India under Muslim Kings. The rise and fall of Ghaznawids. Delhi, Idarah-i-Adabiyat-i-Delhi, 1972.

M. d. c. Lodis

Halim, Abdul
History of the Lodi Sultans of Delhi and Agra. Delhi, Idarah-i-Adabiyat-i-Delhi, 1974.

M. d. d. Pathans

Ambashthya, B.P.
Decisive battles of Sher Shah. Patna. Janaki Prakashan, 1977.

Sensarma, P.
The military profile of Sher Shah Sur. Calcutta. Naya Prakash, 1976.

Siddiqi, Iqtidar H.
History of Sher Shah Suri. Aligarh, P.C. Dwads Shreni, 1971.

Thomas, Edward
Chronicles of the Pathan Kings of Delhi: With a supplement on the revenue resource of the Moghul Empire. New York, Coronet Books, 1985 (Rpt.)

M. d. e. Slave Kings

Ahmad, Muhammad Aziz
Political history and institutions of the early Turkish Empire of Delhi, 1206-1290 A.D. New Delhi, Oriental Books Reprint Corp., 1972.

Joshi, Rekha
Reign of Sultan Balban. Delhi, Ravi Pubs. 1982.

Keene, Henry G.
Turks in India. Delhi, Oriental Pubs. 1972.

Topa, Ishwara.
Politics in pre-Mughal times: A study in the political psychology of the Turkish kings of Delhi up to circa 1400 A.D. Delhi. Idarah-i-Adabiyat-i Delli, 1976. (1A.D. series 33)

M. d. f. Tughluq's

Ahmed, Manazir
Sultan Firoz Shah Tughluq, 1351-1388 A.D. Allahabad, Chugh, 1978.

Husain, Agha Mahdi
Rise and fall of Muhammad Bin Tughluq. Idarah-i-Adabiyat-i-Delhi, 1972.

Tughluq dynasty. New Delhi, S. Chand, 1976.

Jauhri, R. C.
Firoz Tughluq. Agra. Shiv Lal Agarwal, 1970.

Lal, Shiv.
The Sher-Tughluq of India. New Delhi. Newman Group, 1977.

Tughluq of India. Delhi, Newman Group of Pubs; 1977.

M. e. Modern India
M. e. a. General

Chhabra, G. S
Advanced study in the history of modern India. 3 v.Ed 4. V 1.1707-1813 V 2.1814-1919 V 3.1920-1947) New Delhi, Sterling, 1984.

Mahajan V.D.
History of modern India (1919-1982) Volume 1 (1919 to 1974) Delhi, Chand, 1983.

India since 1526. New Delhi, S. Chand, 1976.

Nanda, B.R.
Essays in modern India history. New Delhi, OUP, 1980.

Sharma, Sri Ram
Making of modern India; from A.D. 1526 to the present day. New Delhi, Orient Lengman, 1970.

M. e. b. Mughals
M. e. b. a. General

Agarwal, Ashwani
Studies in Mughal history. Delhi, Motilal Banarsidass, 1984.

Akhtar, M Saleem
Sind under the Mughals. Islamabad, National Institute of Historical & Cultural Research, 1989.

Ansari, M Azhar
European travellers under the Mughals. Delhi, Idara-i-Adabiyat-i-Delhi, 1974.

Aziz, Abdul
Imperial library of the Mughals. Delhi, Idara-i-Adabiyat-e-Dilli, 1974.

Imperial treasury of the Indian Mughals. Delhi, Vishal, 1971.

Batra, Raveendra N.
The downfall of capitalism and communism: A new study of history. London. Macmillan Press, 1978 (includes Khilgis, Tughluqs, Mughals and the Muslim Khatrian era. the Mughal-Maratha Vipran era).

Dutta, S.C.
North—East and the Mughals (1661-1714). New Delhi, D.K. Publishers, Distributors, 1984.

Garrett, H L D and Edwardes S M
Mughal rule in India. New Delhi, S Chand, 1974.

Gascoigne, Bamber
Great Moghuls, Delhi, B I Pub., 1971.

Guha, J. P
Robert Orme: Historical fragments of the Mughal Empire. Delhi, Associated, 1984.

Habib, Irfan
Atlas of the Mughal Empire: Political and economic maps with detailed notes, bibliography and index. Aligarh, Aligarh Muslim Univ., 1982.

Holden, Edward Singleton, ed.
Mogul Emperors of Hindustan, A D 1398-1707. Delhi Metropolitan, 1975.

Mogul emperors of Hindustan, New Delhi, Metropolitan, 1984

Iqbalnama by an anonymous contemporary writer. Tr. S.H. Askari. Patna, Janaki Prakashan 1983. (Persian chronicle of the Mughals, 1712-46)

Ishwari Prasad
Mughal Empire. Allahabad, Chugh Pub., 1974.

Jaffar, S.M.
Mughal Empire from Babar to Aurangzeb. Delhi, Ess. Pub., 1974.

Jones, Dalu
Mirror of princes: The Mughals & the medice. Bombay (N.P.), 1987.

Kapur, G. S.
Refresher course: Mughal rule. 1526-1707. New Delhi. S. Chand, 1970.

Kenedy, Pringle
History of the Great Mughals Delhi, Anmol, 1987.

Kennell, James
Memoirs of a map of Hindustan of the Mogul empire. Calcutta, Editions Indian, 1976.

Kulkarni, G. T.
Mughal-Maratha relations: Twentyfive fateful years. Poona, Publication Dept. Deccan College, 1984.

Lane-Poole, Stanley
History of the Mughal Emperors of Hindustan. Delhi, Oriental Pubs., 1972.

Mahajan. V.D.
Mughal rule in India. 1526-1707. New Delhi, S. Chand, 1970.

Majumdar, R. C.
Mughal empire. Bombay, Bharatiya, 1976.

Marshall, D.N.
Mughals in India: A Bibliographical survey of manuscripts. London, Mansell, 1985.

Mathur, R. S.
Relations of Hadas: with Mughal emperors, 1568-1720 A.D. Delhi, Deputy Publication, 1986.

Mattoo, Abdul Majid
Kashmir under the Mughals, 1586-1752. Srinagar, (n.p.) 1988.

Schimmel, Annemarie, et al
Emperor's album: Images of Mughal India., (n.p.) Abrams, 1987.

Sharma, L.P.
Mughal empire. New Delhi, Konark Publisher, 1987.

Sharma, Sri Ram
Bibliography of Moghul India, A.D. 1526-1767. Bombay, Karnatak Publishing House, 1970.

Sharma, S.R.
Mughal empire in India. Agra, Lakshmi Narain Agarwal, 1972.

Sinha, Surendra N.
Subah of Allahabad under the Great Mughals, 1580-1707. New Delhi, Jamia Milla Islamia, 1974.

Srivastava, M.P.
Policies of the Great Mughals. Allahabad, Chugh, 1978.

Suri, V. S.
Hemu. Patiala, Punjabi Univ., 1970.

Walia, J Mohan
Mughal Empire in India. New Delhi, D.K. Publishers, 1988.

Waller, John H
Niccolo Manucci: A venetian's odyssey in Moghul India, (n.p) International. Univ. Press, 1984.

M. e. b. b. Babur, Mohammad Zahiruddin (d.1530)

Babar, Zahiruddin
Babur-nama:Memoris of Babur. Tr. from Turkish by A.S. Beveridge, New Delhi, Oriental Books Reprint Corpn., 1970

Memoirs of Babar. Abridgement by F.G. Talbit. Delhi, Ess. Ess. Pub., 1974.

Edwards, S. M
Babur-Diarist and despot. New Delhi, Heritage, 1977.

Grenard, Fernand
Babar: first of the Moghals, Dehardun, Natraj, 1971.

Hasan, Muhibul
Babar: founder of the Mughal Empire in India. Ist Edn. New Delhi. Manohar, 1985.

Jena, Krishnachandra,
Baburnama and Babur. Delhi: Sundeep Prakashan, 1978.

Khan, Yusuf, Husain
Two studies in early Mughal history. Simla, IIAS, 1976.

Khan, Zain
Tabqat-i-Baburi Tr. Hasan Askari; Annotation: B.P. Ambastha. Delhi, Idarah-i-Adabiyat-i-Delhi, 1982 (IAD Oriental Services, 19)

Lal, Muni
Babar: life and time. New Delhi, Vikas, 1977.

Lane-Poole, Stanley
Babar. Delhi, S. Chand, 1970.

Palsokar R.D.
Babar: A study in generalship. Poona, Author, 1971.

Shyam, Radhey.
Babar. Patna: Janaki Prakashan, 1978.

Streusand, D.E.
Formation of the Mughal Empire. New Delhi, O.U.P., 1989.

M. e. b. c. Humayun, Muhammad (d. 1556),

Begam, Gulbadan
History Humayun: Humayun nama. Tr. by A. S. Beveridge., Delhi, Oriental Pubs. 1972.

Erskine, William
History of India under Humayun. New Delhi, Metropolitan Book Co., (Distributor), 1987.

Lal, Muni
Humayun. New Delhi, Vikas, 1978.

M. e. b. d. Akbar the Great, Mohammad Jalaluddin (d.1605)

Abu al-Fazl, Ibn Mubarak
Ain-i-Akbari. Tr. H. Blochmann Lahore: Qausain, 1975 (rpt)
Akbarnamah. ed. by Maulawi Abdur Rahim v. 1. Delhi, Kitab Pub. House, 1977.

Afonso, C.J., ed.
Letters from the Mughal Court; the first Jesuit mission to Akbar (1580-1583). Bombay; Heras Institute 1980

Agarwal, C.M.
Akbar and his Hindu Officers; A critical study. Jalandhar: A B S Publications, 1986.

Agustus, F and Beveridge, A. S
Emperor Akbar.2 V. Patna, Association Book Agency, 1980.

Ambashthya, B. P. ed.
Contributions on Akbar and the Parsees (Reprint of articles by R.P. Karkaria and J.J. Modi published in J. B. B. R. A. S (1896-1903). Patna. Janaki Prakashan, 1976.

Beveridge, A. S
Emperor Akbar: A contribution towards the history of India. Delhi, Academic Asiatica, 1973.

Brand, Michael, ed.
Fatehpur Sikri. New Delhi, Mars Pub., 1987.

Brand, M and G.D. Lowry
Akbar and Fatehpur Sikri. Bombay, Marg. Pub., 1987.

Dujarrio, Pierre
Akbar and Jesuits: an account of the Jesuit mission to the court of Akbar. Tr. by C.B. Payne. New Delhi, Tulsi Pub. House, 1979.

Khan, Kunwar, R.A
Kachhwahas under Akbar and Jahangir. New Delhi, Kitab Bhavan, 1976.

Lal, Muni
Akbar, New Delhi, Vikas, 1980.

Lane-Pool, Stanley
Medieval India from the Mohammedan conquest to the reign of Akbar the Great. The United Empire — Akbar the Great to the Fall of Moghul Empire — The Hindu Revival, 1707—1765 A.D. New Delhi, Asian Educational Service, 1986.

Malleson, G.B
Akbar and the rise of Mughal empire. Ambala Cantt. Bhagi Pubs. 1972.

Moreland, William Harrison
India at the death of Akbar. New Delhi, Oriental Books, 1984.

Noer, Friedrick Christian Karl Augusty
Emperor Akbar, contribution towards the history of India in the 16th century. Tr. by A.S. Beveridge.2 V. Patna, Academica Asiaticam, 1973.

Qureshi, Ishtiaq H., and Iqtidar H Qureshi
Akbar — The Architect of the Mughal Empire.
Delhi, Idarah-i-Adabiyat-i-Delhi, 1987.

M. e. b. e. Jahangir, Mohammad Nooruddin (Saleem, d. 1627)

Lal, Muni
Jahangir. New Delhi, Vikas, 1983.

M. e. b. f. Shahjahan, Khurram Shihabuddin Muhammad, (d. 1666)

Lal, Muni
Shahjahan. New Delhi, Vikas Pub. House, 1986.

Fanshawe, H.C.
Shahjahan's Delhi: Past and present (Illustrated). Delhi, Sumit Prakashan, 1979.

M.e.b.g. Aurangzeb, Alamgir, Muhiyuddin (d. 1707)

Agrawal, C.M.
Wazirs of Aurangzeb, Bodh—Gaya: Kanchan Pub., 1978.

Ahmad, Laiq
Prime Minister of Aurangzeb. Allahabad, Chugh, 1976.

Chaturbhuj
Great historical dramas: The Lion of Maharashtra and last Mughal emperor. New Delhi, Metropolitan Book Co. Distributor, 1987.

Farukhi, Zahiruddin
Aurangzeb and his Times. Delhi. Idarah-i-Adabiyat-i-Delhi, 1972.

Hallissey, Robert C.
The Rajput rebellion against Aurangzeb: A study of the Mughal Empire in seventeenth century India. Columbia, U. of Missouri Press, 1977.

Hunter, William Wilson
Aurangzeb. New Delhi, S. Chand, 1970.

Joshi, Rekha
Aurangzeb: Attitudes and inclination. New Delhi, Munshiram Manoharlal, 1979.

Kashmiri, Inayatallah Khan
Kalimat-i-taiyibat (Collection of Aurangzeb's Orders). Edited by S.M. Azizuddin Husain. Delhi: Idarah-i-Adabiyat-i-Delhi, 1982 (IAD Oriental Serices. 23) (Persian text with English introd. & translation of selected passages)

Lal, Muni
Augangzeb. New Delhi, Vikas, 1989

Lane-Poole, Stanley
Aurangzeb and the decay of the Mughal Empire. Delhi, S.Chand, 1970.

Nagar, Ishwar Das
Futuhat-i-Alamgiri. Tr. and edited by Tasneem Ahmad. Delhi, Idarah-i-Adabiyat-i-Delhi, 1978.

Sarkar, Sir Jadunath
Anecdotes of Aurangzeb (English translation of Akham-i-Alamgiri, Calcutta, Orient Longman, 1988.

A shorty history of Aurangzeb. New Delhi, Orient Longman, 1979.

Syed, Anees Jahan
Aurangzeb in Muntakhab-al-Lubab. Bombay, Somaiya, 1977.

Tripathi, R.P.
Rise and fall of the Mughal Empire: Aurangzeb to later Mughals. Allahabad, Central Book Depot, 1987.

M.e.b.h. Later Mughals

Alam, Muzaffar
Crisis of empire in Mughal North India: Awadh and the Punjab (1707-1748). Calcutta, O.U.P., 1986.

Fraser, James
History of Nadir Shah Delhi. Mohan Pub., 1973.

Francklin, W
History of Shah Alam. New Delhi. Classical Pub. Co., 1983.

Gupta, Hari Ram
Later Mughal history of the Punjab (1707-1793). Lahore: Sang-e-meel Publications, 1976.

Gupta, Praful Chandra
Shah Alam II and his court. Calcutta, Mukhopadhya, 1970.

Husain, Mahdi
Bahadur Shah, New Delhi, Metropolitan Book Co., Distributor, 1988.

Irvine, William
Later Mughals. Edited and augmented with the history of Nadirshah's invasion by Jadunath Sarkar. Ed.2. New Delhi, Oriental Book Reprinters, 1971.

Keene, Henry G.
Fall of the Mughal empire. Delhi, Oriental Publishers, 1971.

Khosla, G. D
Last Moghul. New Delhi, Navrang, 1986.

Lane-Poole, Stanley
History of India from the reign of Akbar the Great to the fall of the Mughal Empire. New York, AMS Press, 1970 (rpt)

Sarkar, Jadunath
Fall of the Mughal Empire. Delhi, Orient Longman, 1971.

Nadir Shah in India. Calcutta. Naya Prakash, 1973.

M.e.c British Rule

Ali, Shanti Sadiq
India and Africa through the ages. New Delhi, National Book Trust, 1987.

Anderson, G and M Subedar
Expansion of British India. New Delhi, Uppal, 1986.

Aziz, K
British in India: A study in imperialism. Islamabad, National Institute of Historical & Cultural Research, 1976.

Banerjee, A.C.
Eastern frontier of British India, 1784-1826. Calcutta: K P Bagchi, 1986.

Bava, P. S.
Memories of the Raj. Delhi, Hind Pocket Books, 1981.

Bayly, C.A. and D.H.A. Kalff
Two colonial empires: India and Indonesia in the 19th century (Comparative Studies in Overseas History). Dordrecht, Netherlands, Nijhoff, 1986.

Bhattacharjee, Arun
History of modern India 1757—1947. New Delhi, Ashish Pub. House, 1976.

Bilgrami, Saghir H
Afghanistan and British India, 1793—1907: A study in foreign Relations. New Delhi, Sterling, 1972.

Blusse, L. et al.
India and Indonesia from the 1920s to the 1950s: The Origins of Planning. (Comparative History of India and Indonesia, 1) Leiden, Brill, 1987.

Chudgar, P. L
Indian Princes under British Protection. New Delhi, Skylark Pub., 1986.

Darby, Philip
Three faces to Imperialism: British and American Approaches to Asia and Africa, 1870—1970. New Haven, Yale Univ. Press, 1987.

Ghosh, B
British policy towards the Pathans and the Pindaris in Central India, 1805-1818. Calcutta, Punthi Pustak, 1970.

Heyday of colonial Rule: India and Indonesia from 1830s to 1914s. Leiden, Brill, 1987.

Hunter, William. W.
From the First European settlement to the founding of the English East India Company. v 6 & 7. New Delhi, AES, 1987.

India and Indonesia during the 17th and 18th centuries. Leiden, Brill, 1988.

Mukhopadhayay, Theodore S.C.
British Residents at the Darbar of Bengal Nawabs of Murshidabad, 1757-1772. New Delhi, Metropolitan Book Co. (Distributors), 1988.

Murthy, K.V.S.
Kohinoor in the Crown. New Delhi, Metropolitan Book Co. (Distributor), 1987.

Varma, Birendra
From Delhi to Teheran: A study of British diplomatic moves in North—Western India, Afghanistan and Persia 1772—1803. Patna, Janaki Prakashan, 1980.

Yapp, M. E
Strategies of British India, British Iran and Afghanistan 1798-1850 Calcutta, OUP, 1980.

M.e.d. Eighteen — Fifty Seven (1857)

Anand, Mulkraj
Truth about the 1857 Revolt: The otherside of the medal. New Delhi, Metropolitan Book Co., distributor), 1988.

Ball, Charles
History of the Indian mutiny: Giving a detailed account of the sepoy insurrection in India and a concise history of the great military events which have tended to consolidate British Empire in Hindustan, 2 V. New Delhi, Master Pubs., 1981.

Broehl, Wayne G
Crisis of the Raj: The revolt of 1857 through British Lieutenants eyes, U Pr. of New England, 1986.

Chandra, S.N.
1857: Some untold stories. New Delhi, Sterling Publishers, 1976.

Chaudhuari, S. Bhusan
English historical writings on the Indian Mutiny 1857-1859. Calcutta, World Press, 1979.

Chathopadhyaya B. P
Sepoy munity 1857; A social study and analysis. Calcutta, Mukhopadyay, 1970.

Datta, K.K. and V.A. Narain
Comprehensive history of India V.11 consolidation of British rule in India 1818-1858. Delhi, People's Pub. House, 1985 (includes Sepoy Mutiny)

Devi, Ritambhari
Indian mutiny 1857 in Bihar. New Delhi, Chetna, 1980.

Domin, Dolores
India in 1857--59; A study in the role of the Sikhs in the people's uprising. Berlin: Akademic Verlag, 1977 (Studies of Asia, Africa, and Latin America, 17)

Dutt, B. C
Mutiny of the Innocents. Bombay. Sindhu Pub., 1971.

Dutt, Utpal Tr.
Great rebellion, 1857 Tr. by the Author. Calcutta, Seagull Books, 1986.

Edwards, A.M
Season in Hell., (n.p) Taplingers, 1973.

Ernbree A.
India in 1857: The revolt against foreign rule. New Delhi, Metropolitan Book Co. (Distributor), 1987.

Fuller, J. F. C
India in revolt. New Delhi: Discovery, 1985.

Ghosh, Pramita
Meerut conspiracy case and the left wing in India. Calcutta, Papyrus, 1978.

Henry, W.
Delhi — 1857. New Delhi, Metropolitan Book Co. (Distributor), 1988.

Hibbert, Christopher
The great mutiny India: 1857., London: Allen Lane, 1978.

India; National Archives.
Descriptive list of Mutiny papers in the National Archives of India, Bhopal.V. III. Delhi, Manager of Pub., 1970.

ss
Jacob, G.L.
Western India Before and during the Mutinies. (n.p), Mayur Pubs. Indian, 1985 (rpt)

Joshi, PC. ed.
Rebellion 1857: A symposium. Calcutta. K.P. Bagchi & Co. 1986.

Kaye, J. W
Kaye's and Malleson's History of the Indian Mutiny of 1857—58. 6 vols. Ed. George B. Malleson. Greenwood 1971.

Keene, Henry G.
British administration during the revolt of 1857. New Delhi, IIP 1985.

Khan, Sir Syed Ahmad
History of the Bijnor Rebellion Tr. from Urdu by Hafeez Malik. Delhi, Idarah-i-Adabiyat-i-Delhi, 1982.

Koya, J.W.
History of the great revolt, in 3 vols. New Delhi, Metropolitan Book Co. (Distributor), 1988.

Mead, Henry.
Sepoy Revolt. Its causes, and its consequences. New Delhi: Gian Pub. House, 1986.

Mills, Arthur
India in 1858. New Delhi, Gian, 1986.

Mukherjee, Rudrangshu
Awadh in revolt 1857—1858: A study of popular resistance. New Delhi, OUP, 1984.

Norman, Henry W. Ed.
Delhi 1857. The Siege assault and capture as given in the diary correspondence of the late Colonel Keith Young. Delhi, Gian, 1987.

Rawding, F.W.
The Rebellion in India, 1857. London: Cambridge U.P., 1977 (Cambridge introduction in the history of makind-topic book)

Roberts, Abraham
Eye witness account of the India mutiny. Delhi, Mittal, 1984.

Roton, J.E.W.
Meerut Mutiny and the seige of Delhi. Guwahati, (N.P.) 1989 (rpt)

Sen, Surendra Nath
Eighteen Fifty seven New Delhi, Publications., Division., 1977.

Seton, Rosemary
Indian 'Mutiny' 1857—1858:A guide to source material in the Indian Office Library and Records. London: The British Library, 1986.

Srivastava, M.P
Indian Mutiny, 1857. Allahabad, Chug, 1979.

Stokes E and C.A. Bayly
Peasant armed: The Indian revolt of 1857. New Delhi, O.U.P., 1986.

Wilberforce, G .
Unrecorded chapter of the Indian mutiny. Being the personal reminisces of Rejinad G. Wilberforce. Gurgaon, Academic Press, 1978.

Yadav, K. C. Ed.
Delhi in 1857. V. 1. Gurgaon, Academic Press, 1980.

M.e.f. Freedom Movement:

Ahad, Abdul

Kashmir to frankfurt: A study of arts and crafts with a chapter on the freedom struggle of Kashmir, New Delhi: Rima Pub. House, 1987.

Ahluwalia B.K. and S. Ahluwalia
Muslims and India's freedom movement. New Delhi, Heritage, 1986.

Ahmed, Jamiluddin, Cpmp
Historic documents of Muslim in freedom movements. Lahore, United Pub., 1970.

Ahmad, Karuna C
Gandhi, Women's roles and the freedom movement. New Delhi. Nehru Memorial Museum and Library, 1986.

Ahmed, Mesbahaddin
British labour party and the Indian independence movement 1917—1939. New Delhi: Sterling, Publishers, 1987.

Allana, G.
Eminent Muslim freedom fighters, 1562-1947, Twentyone great lives. Delhi, Neeraj, 1983 (rpt)

Bahadur, K.P.
History of the Freedom movement in India, v.2. New Delhi, Ess Ess Pub., 1987.

Bedi, Kiran
Demand for Swaraj (1905-1930). Jalandhar, ABS Publications, 1985.

Bhargava, Motilal
Role of press in the freedom movement. New Delhi, Reliance Publication, 1987.

Chinnian, P
Vellore mutiny, 1806—the first uprising against the British.

Madras, Chinnian, 1982.

Chopra, P.N.
Role of Indian Muslims in the struggle for freedom. New Delhi, Light and Life, 1979.

Collins, Larry and D. Lapierre
Freedom at midnight. New Delhi, Vikas, 1976.

Dutta, Abhijit
Muslim society in transition: Titu Meer's Revolt (1831) A study. Calcutta, Minerra, 1987.

Datta, K. K
Anti British plots and movements before 1857. Meerut, Meenakshi, 1970.

Engineer, Asghar Ali.
Role of minorities in freedom struggle. New Delhi, Ajanta, 1986.

Gajra, Baldev. T.
Sind's role in the freedom struggle. Bombay, The Author, 1986.

Gubbins, M. R
Mutinies in Oudh. Patna, Janaki Prakashan, 1978.

Guha, A. C
First spark of revolution. New Delhi, Orient Longman, 1970.

History of the freedom movement: Being the study of Muslim struggle for freedom of Hind—Pakistan 1907—1947 in 4 Vols. Karachi, Pakistan Historical society, 1984 (rpt)

Imam, M. M
Role of Muslims in the national movement 1912-1930: A study of Bihar. New Delhi, Mittal, 1987.

Khan, G. H
Freedom Movement in Kashmir, 1931—40. New Delhi, Light

and Life Pubs., 1980.

Khan, M. Raza
What Price Freedom? (N.P.) The Author, 1970.

Khilnani, N.M
India's road to independence, 1857 to 1947: Panorama of India's struggle for freedom. New Delhi, Sterling. Publishers, 1987.

Lal, Pandit Sunder
How India lost her freedom. Bombay, Popular, 1970.

Madan, Som Nath
Freedom movement in India: A select bibliography. Delhi, Anmol Publications, 1987.

Muhammad, Shan
Freedom movement in India: The role of Ali Brothers. New Delhi, Associated, 1983.

Khaksar movement in India. Meerut, Meenakshi, 1972.

Puri, Harish K.
Ghadar movement: ideology strategy & organisation. Amritsar, Gurunanak Dev Univ., 1983.

Ray, Santimay
Freedom movement and Indian Muslims. New Delhi. People's Pub. House, 1970.

Role of India Muslims in the freedom movement.New Delhi, People's Pub. House, 1971.

Rushdie, Salman
Midnight children. New York, Knopf, 1981.

Sadiq, Mohammad
Turkish revolution & the Indian freedom movement. New Delhi, Macmillan, 1984.

Sharma, Kamlesh
Role of Muslims in Indian politics 1857—1947. New Delhi, Radiant, 1986.

Yasin, Mohammad and A.Q. Rafaqi, ed.
History of the freedom struggle in Jammu and Kashmir. New Delhi, Light and Life, 1980.

Yunus, Mohammad
Frontier Pathans and freedom struggle. Delhi, Anmol Pub., 1985.

M.e.g. Specific Geographical Areas
M.e.g.a. North India.
M.e.g.a 1. Agra

Gupta, I.P.
Urban glimpses of Mughal India: Agra the Imperial capital, 16th & 17th centuries. Delhi. Discovery Publishing House, 1986.

Lall, Janardan Shankar
Taj Mahal and the glory of Mughal Agra; Text by John L Lall, Photographs by DN Dube. Varanasi, Lustre Press, 1982.

Latif, S.M.
Agra: Historical and descriptive. Jaipur, Historical Research Documentation Programme (Distributor), 1981.

Marehravi, Said Ahmed.
Monuments of Agra: Historical study. Tr.R. Nath. Jaipur, Historical Research Documentation Programme 1989.

Nath, R.
Agra and its monumental glory. Bombay, Taraporevala, 1977.

Rizvi, Saiyid Athar Abbas and V.J.A. Flynn.

Fathepur Sikri. Bombay: Taraporevala, 1979.

M.e.g.a 2: Bengal

Bose, S.
Agrarian Bengal: Economy, social structure and Politics, 1919—1947. (Cambridge South Asian Studies). Leiden, Brill, 1986.

Ibn Battuta,
Ibn Battuta's account of Bengal. Tr. into English by Harinath De. Calcutta, Prajana, 1978.

Roy, A.C.
History of Bengal: Turko-Afghan period. New Delhi, Kalyani, 1986.

Sarkar, Jadunath
History of Bengal: Muslim period, 1200-1757. Patna, Janaki Prakashan, 1977.

M.e.g.a 3: BIHAR

Ahmad, Qayamuddin
Corpus of Arabic and Persian inscriptions of Bihar, A.D. 640-1200. Patna, K.P. Jayaswal Research Institute, 1973.

Askari, Syed Hasan & Qeyamuddin Ahmed, Ed.
Comprehensive history of Bihar, V.2. Patna: Kashi Prasad Jayaswal Research Institute, 1976. (Historical Research series, XIV).

M.e.g.a 4: DELHI

Chopra, P
Delhi: History and places of interest. Delhi, Administration, 1970.

Dayal, Maheshwar.
Rediscovering Delhi: The story of Shahjahanbad. Delhi, S. Chand, 1982.

Frykenberg, R.E.
Delhi through the ages: Essays in urban history, culture, and society. New Delhi, O.U.P., 1986.

Gupta, Narayan
Delhi between two Empires. 1803—1931: Society, government and urban growth. Delhi, Oxford University Press, 1981.

Khan, Sir Syed Ahmed,
Athar al Sanadid. (Monuments of Delhi: A historical study) Tr. R. Nath. Jaipur, Historical Documentation Research Programme, 1987.

Llewellyn, Alexander.
The siege of Delhi. London: Macdonald & Jane's. 1977.

Mitra, Ashok.
Delhi: capital city. New Delhi, Thomson Press, 1970.

Monuments of Delhi. A historicals study. New Delhi, Ambika, 1981.

Singh, Kushwant and Raghu Rai.
Delhi: A portrait. New Delhi, Central News Agency, 1983.

Stephen, Carr.
Archaeology and monumental remains of Delhi. New Delhi, Ashish Pub. House, 1976.

M.e.g.a 5: GUJARAT

Gokhale, Balkrishna Govind.
Surat in the Seventeenth Century: A study in urban history of

pre—modern India. London: Curzon Press, 1979. (Scandinavian Inst. of Asian Studies monograph series, 28.)

Khan, A. Mohammed.
Medieval Gujarat: Its political and statistical history based on Mirat-i-Ahmadi. Tr. James Bird. Delhi, Indian Bibliographies Bureau, 1985.

Kidman, B.
Once upon a far hillside: the life and times of an Indian village. London: Century, 1985. (Borli Panchatan, Muslim & Hindu village on the coast of Maharashtra.)

Malik, Zahiruddin.
Reign of Muhammad Shah, 1719-1748. Bombay, Asia, 1977.

M.e.g.a 6: KASHMIR

Ahmad, Hussam-ud-din,
Islam in Kashmir, 1320-1819. London, International Institute of Kashmir Studies, 1987.

Ahmad, S. Maqbul and R. Bano
Historical Geography of Kashmir: Based on Arabic and Persian sources from AD 800-1900. Delhi, Ariana Pub. House, 1984.

Bamzai, P.N.K
Socio-Economic History of Kashmir. New Delhi, Metropolitan, 1987.

Chhabra, G.S and Charak, S. D. S.
Jammu & Kashmir: Aspect of socio-political history. New Delhi, Archives Publishers, 1986.

Dogra, Ramesh Chander
Jammu and Kashmir: A select and annotated bibliography of manuscripts, books and articles together with a survey of its history, languages and literature from Rajatarangini to modern times. Delhi, Ajanta Pub., 1986.

Kapur, M. L
History of Medieval Kashmir, 1320-1586 AD. Jammu, A R B Pub. 1981.

Rabbani, G.M.
Kashmir, Social and Cultural History. Ed.1. Delhi, Anmol Publishers, 1986.
Studies in History and Culture of Kashmir. Jammu, Trikuta pub., 1976.

Sufi, G.M.D.
Kashmir: Beeing a History of Kashmir from the Earliest Times to our own. New Delhi, Light and Life Publishers, 1974.

Zutshi, N.K.
Sultan Zain-ul-Abidin of Kashmir, an age of enlightenment. Jammu, Nupur Prakashan, 1976.

M.e.g.a 7: Lucknow

Ahad, Abdul.
Tarikh Badshah Begam: A Persian manuscript on the history of Oudh. Tr. Muhammed Taqui Ahmed. Delhi: Idara-i-Adabiyat-i-Delhi, 1977.

Ahmad, Safi
Two kings of Awadh: Muhammed Ali Shah and Amjad Ali Shah, 1837-47. Aligarh, P.C. Dwadesh Shreni, 1971.

Basu, Purendu
Oudh and the East India Company. Allahabad, Kitabistan, 1970.

Khan, Mirza A. Talib
History of Asafud-Daulah: Nawab of Oudh, being a translation of events with his administration. Tr. from Persian by WL Hoey. Lucknow, Pustak Kendra, 1971.

Kumar, Kapil
Peasants in revolt: Tenants, landords, Congress and the Raj in Oudh. New Delhi, Manohar, 1984.

Llewellyn-Jones, Rosie
Fatal friendship: The Nawabs, the British and the City of Lucknow. New Delhi, OUP. 1985.

Oldenburg, V.T.
The making of colonial Lucknow 1856-1877. Prinecton: Preinceton University Press, 1984.

Pemble, John Charles.
Raj, the Indian mutiny and the kingdom of Oudh, 1801-1859. Delhi, OUP, 1979.

Sarvadhikari, Raj K.
Taluqdari settlement in Oudh. Delhi, Usha 1986

Singhal, Damodar P.
British relations with Oudh, 1801-1857: A case study. Calcutta, KP Bagchi, 1983.

Srivastava, A.L.
First two Nawabs of Awadh. Ed. 2. Agra, Shiv Lal Agarwal, 1970.
M.e.g.a 8: Orissa

Haque, M.A.
Muslim administration in Orissa (1568-1751 A.D.). Calcutta: Punthi Pustak, 1980. (Orissan Studies project, Nr.8).

Ray, B.C.
Orissa under the Mughals: From Akbar to Avlivardi: A fascinating study of the socio-economic and cultural history of Orissa. Calcutta, Punthi Pustak, 1983.

M.e.g.b *South India*:

M.e.g.b 1. ***General***

Aiyangar, S.
South India and her Muhammadan invaders, Delhi, S. Chand, 1971.

Chopra (P.N.) et.al.
History of South India. 3V.
—V 1. Ancient period.
—V 2. Medieval period.
—V 3. Modern period.
New Delhi, S. Chand, 1979.

Ramaswami, N.S.
Political history of Carnatic under the Nawabs. New Delhi, Abhinay 1984.

Sastri, Nilakanta
History of South India: From prehistoric to the fall of Vijayanagar. Ed. 4. Madras, OUP. 1983

Wilks, Mark and M. Hammick, ed.
Historical sketches of South Indian history from the earliest times to the last Mohammedan Dynasty. 4 vols. Coronet Bks. 1977 (Rpt.)

M.e.g.b 2: Deccan

Alavi, R, Ahmed.
Studies in the History of Medieval Deccan. Delhi, Idarai-Adab-iyat-i-Delhi, 1977.

Bawa, V. Kumar.
Aspects of Deccan History: Report of a Seminar. Hyderabad, Inst. of Asian Studies, 1975.

Bhandarkar, Ramakrishna Gopal
Early history of the Dekkan down to the Mohammedan conquest. Ed. 2. New Delhi, Asian Educational Services, 1979.

Khalidi, Omar.
Dakan (Deccan) under the Sultans, 1296-1724: A Bibliography of monographic and periodical literature. Wichita, KS: Hayderabad Historical Society, 1987.

Nayeem, M.A.
External relations of the Bijapur Kingdom, 1489-1686. Hyderabad British Pub. 1975.

Sathyanarayana, K
Study of the history and culture of the Andhras. V 5: The Delhi, Sultanate (1206-1526). New Delhi, PPH, 1983.

Sherwani, H.K. and Joshi, P. M. Ed.
History of Medieval Deccan, 1295-1725.V 1. Hyderabad, Govt. of AP Press, 1973.

Verma, D C.
History of Bijapur. Delhi, Rajesh Pub, 1973.

Yazdani, Ghulam, Ed.
Early History of the Deccan, 2V. New Delhi, Munshiram Manoharlal, 1981.

Megb 3: Hyderabad

Aleem, Shamim and M.A.Aleem, ed.
Developments in administration under H.E.H. Nizam VII. Hyderabad, The Author, 1984.

Ansari, N.H.
Chronicles of the seize of Golconda Fort. Delhi, Idara-i-Habiyat-i-Delli, 1975.

Bawa, Vasant Kumar.
Nizam between Mughals and British: Hyderabad under Salar Jung I. New Delhi, S. Chand. 1986.

Bilgrami, S.A.A.
Landmarks of the Deccan: A comprehensive guide to the

archeological remains of the City and Suburbs of Hyderabad. New Delhi, Madras 1984.

Briggs, H.G.
Nizam: History and relations with the British Government. 2. V. Delhi, Manas Pub. 1985.

Fraser, Hastings
Our faithful ally, the Nizam. Delhi, Modern Publishers and Distributors. 1985.

Kate, P.V.
Marathwada under the Nizams. Delhi, Mittal, 1987.

Khalidi, Omer
Hayderabad State under the Nizam, 1724-1948: A bibliography of monographic and periodical literature. Wichtia, Hayderabad Society, 1986.

Prasad, Dharmendra
Social and cultural geography of Hyderabad City. New Delhi, Indian, 1986.

Prasad, Rajendra
Asif Jahs of Hyderabad: Their rise and decline. New Delhi, Vikas 1984.

Raj, Sheela
Medievalism to modernism: socio-economic & cultural history of Hyderabad 1869-1911. New Delhi, Popular Prakashan, 1987.

Reddy, V. Ramakrishna
Economic history of Hyderabad state: Warangal Saba. 1911-1950 Delhi: Gian Pub. House, 1987.

Regani, Sarojini
Nizam British Relations 1724-1857. New Delhi, Concept, 1989.

Richards, J.F.

Mughal administration in Golconda. London. Oxford U.P., 1976.

Sherwani, H.K.
History of the Qutab Shahi Dynasty. New Delhi, Munshiram Monaharlal, 1974.

Yazdani, Zubaida
Hyderabad during the Residency of Henry Russell. 1811-1820; A case study of the Subsidiary Alliance System. Oxford U.P., 1976.

M.e.g.b. 4: Malabar

Choudhary, Sukbir,
Mopplah uppraising 1921-1923. Delhi, Agam Prakashan, 1977.

Dale, S.F.
Mappilas of Malabar, 1498-1922: Islamic Society on the South Asian frontier. New Delhi, OUP. 1980.

Hardgrave, Robert
Peasent revolt in Malabar. Columbia, South Asia Books, 1981.

Hitchcock, R. H.
History of the Malabar Rebellion, 1921. Delhi. Usha Pub., 1983.

Miller, R.E.
Mappila Muslims of Kerala: A study in Islamic trends. New Delhi, Orient Longmans, 1976.

Panikkar, K.N.
Against Lord and State: Religion and Peasant Uprisings in Malabar (1836-1921). New Delhi, OUP 1988.

Panikkar, T. K. G.
Malabar and its Folk. New Delhi. Asian Educational Services, 1983.

Rajendran, N.P.
Establishment of British Power in Malabar, 1664-1799. Allahabad, Chugh, 1979.

Ramaswami, N.S.
Mamallapuram. An Annotated Bibliography. Madras: New Era Publishers, 1980.

Shah, S. Mohideen
Islam in Kerala. (n.p.) Muslim Education Association. 1977.

Wood, Conard.
Mopplah, Rebellion: Its genesis. New Delhi. People's Pub. House, 1987.

Megb. 5: Mysore

Ali, B. Sheikh
Tipu Sultan: A study in diplomacy and confrontation. Mysore, Geetha Book House 1982.

Azer, Rahman.
Tiger Sultan. Illustrated monograph on Tipu Sultan, Bangalore. Naya Pub. 1982.

Dhar, G. N
Authentic Memoirs of Tipu Sultan. Delhi, Ajanta, 1979.

Dirom, Major.
A narrative of the campaign in India which terminated the war with Tippu Sultan in 1792. New Delhi, Asian Educational Service, 1985.

Gidwani, Bhagwan S.
Sword of Tipu Sultan, Bombay. Allied, 1978.

Gopal, Mysore Batti.
Tipu Sutlan's Mysore: An economic study, Bombay. Popular 1972.

Hasan, Mohibul.
History of Tipu Sultan. Calcutta. World, 1971.

Kalliaurthy. G.
Second Anglo Mysore War 1780-84. New Delhi, Metropolitan Book, Co. (Distributor), 1987.

Kareem, C.K.
Kerala Under Haider Ali and Tipu Sultan. Cochin. Kerala Historical Association, 1973.

Kirmani, Mir H.A.K.
History of Tipu Sultan: Being a continuation of the Nishan-i-Hyduri. Tr. Col. W. Miles. New Delhi, Asian Educational Service, 1986.

Meadows, Taylor.
Tippu Sultan: A Tale of Mysore War. Delhi, Usha, 1986.

Michaud, J.
History of Mysore under Hyder Ali & Tippu Sultan. Tr. by V.K. Raman Menon. New Delhi: Asian Educational Services, 1986.

Mohammad, Gholam .
History of Hyder Ali and Tipu Sultan. New Delhi. Cosmo, 1976.

Muddachari, B.
Resistance of Mysore to Maratha expansion, 1726-1761. Mysore, University of Mysore 1970.

Palsokar, R. D.
Tipu Sultan. Poona, Author, 1970.

Rice, B. Lewis.
Tipu Sultan X rayed. Mysore. Usha Press, 1980.

Taylor, M.
Tippu Sultan: A tale of the Mysore War. New Delhi. Asian Educational Service, 1986.

Tour, Maister Dila.
History of Hyder Shah (Hyder Ali Khan). Delhi. Daya Pub. House, 1986.
Hyder Ali & Revolution in India. Delhi, Cosmo, 1988.

Vatsal, Tulsi,
Tipu Sultan. New Delhi. I.C.C.R., 1985.

M.f. Administrative

Aleem, Shamim
Personal management in Princeley State. New Delhi, Gitanjali, 1985.

Ali, M. Athar
Apparatus of Empire: Awards of ranks, officer and titles to the Mughal nobility, 1574-1658.

Mansab's appointments to offices and titles in the Mughal empire. A conspectus 1574-1658. New Delhi, O.U.O., 1982.

Ansari, M.A.
Administrative documents of Mughal India. New Delhi, BRPC., 1984.

Aziz, Abdul
Mansabdari system and the Mughal army. Delhi, Idara-i-Adabiyat-i-Delhi, 1972.

Bhanu, Dharma
History and administration of the North-Western provinces, 1803-1856. Agra Shiv lal Agarwal, 1970.

Bilgrami, Rafat M
Religious and quasi religious departments of the Mughal Period, 1556-1707. New Delhi, Munshiram Manohharlal, 1983.

British India analysed: The provincial & revenue establishments of Tippoo Sultan and of Mohammadan and British conquerors in Hindustan states. 3 vols. New Delhi, D.K. Publishers, Distributors 1988.

Chand, Tej Pratap
Administration of Avadh, 1858-1877. Varanasi, Vishwavidyalaya Prakasham, 19711.

Chandra, Satish
Medieval India: Society, the jagirdari crisis and the village. New Delhi, Macmillan, 1982.

Day, Upendra Nath
Government of the Sultanate. New Delhi, Rajesh Pub., 1983.
Mughal government, A.D. 1556-1707. New Delhi, Munshiram Manoharlal, 1971.

Dutta, K P
Administrative aspects of medieval institutions in India. Calcutta, J.K. Enterprises, 1973.

Hassan, Ibn
Central structure of the Mughal empire and its practical working upto the year 1657. New Delhi, Munshiram Manoharlal, 1970.

Khan, A.R.
Chieftans in the Mughal Empire during the reign of Akbar. Simla, India Inst. of Advanced Studies, 1977.

Khan Mubarak A
Court of the great Mughals: Based on Persian sources. Lahore, Book Traders, 1986.

Khan, Shah Nawaz and Abdul Hayy.
Maathirul-Umara: Being biographies of the Muhammadan and Hindu officers of the Timurid sovereigns of India. Patna, Janaki Prakasham, 1979.

Moreland, W.H.
Agrarian system of Muslim India. Delhi, Amar Prakasham, 1988 (rpt).

Moosvi, Shireen
Economy of the Mughal Empire c-1595: A statistical study. Oxford, Oxford Univ. Press, 1987.

Nayeem, M.A.
Mughal Administration of Deccan under Nizam-ul-Mulk Asaf Jah. New Delhi, Jaico, 1985.

Qureshi, Ishtiaq H
Administration of the Mughal empire. Patna, Janaki, Prakashan, 1983.

Administration of the Sultanate of Delhi. New Delhi, Munshiram Manoharlal, 1972.

Quraishi, M A
Indian administration: Pre-and post independence: Memoirs of an I.C.S., Delhi, B.R. Pub Corp., 1985.

Rashid, Khalid and Athar Husin
Wakf Law and administration in India ed.2 Delhi, Eastern Book Co. 1973.

Rashid, S. Khalid
Wakf Administration in India: A Socio-legal study New Delhi, Vikas, 1978.

Richards, J.F.ed.
Document forms of official orders of appointment in the Mughal Empire. Cambridge: Gibb Memorial Trust, 1986.

Sarkar, Jadunath
Mughal administration, New Delhi. Orient Longman 1973.

Siddiqi, Noman Ahmed
Land revenue Administration Under the Mughals, 1700-1750 Bombay, Asia, 1970.

Yasin, Madhvi
Indian administration: A study of Indian polity towards end of the nineteenth century. New Delhi Linght & Life, 1979.

Mg. Socio-Economic

Ambirajan.
Classical political economy in British India. New Delhi, Vikas, 1982.

Ansari, M.A
Social life of the Mughal Emperor. New Delhi, Gitajnali Prakashan, 1974.

Banerjee, A. C.
Aspects of Indo-British economic relations, 1858-1898. New Delhi, OUP, 1982.

Bhattacharya, S.
East India Company and the economy of Bengal. Calcutta, Mukhopadhya, 1970.

Chaudhary, Neelam.
Socio-economic history of Mughal India. Delhi, Discovery House, 1987.

Chitnis, K.N.
Socio-economic aspects of medieval India. Poona, Mrs. R.K

Chitnis, 1979.

Chopra, P. K
Society and culture during the Mughal Age. Delhi, Agam, 1987.

Dodwell, Henry.
Nababs of Madras. New Delhi, Asian Education, 1986.

Dua, Shiva S.
Society and Culture in Northern India. Delhi, Indian Bibliographies Bureau 1986.

Engineer, Asghar Ali.
Origin and development of Islam: An essay on its socio-economic growth. New Delhi: Orient Longman, 1980.

Farooque, A.K. Muhammad.
Roads and communications in Mughal India. Delhi, Idara-i-Ababiyat-i-Delhi, 1979.

Fisher, Michael H.
Clash of cultures, Awadh the British and the Mughals. New Delhi, Manohar, 1987.

Gadra, Pramod B.
Cultural archaeology of Ahmadnagar during Nizam Shahi Period, 1494-1632. New Delhi, BRPC, 1986.

Habib, Mohammad
Politics and Society during the Early Medieval Period: Collected works. Ed. K.A. Nizami. 2.v. New Delhi, Prentice Hall of India, 1981.

Hasan, Saiyid Nurul
Thoughts on agrarian relations in Mughal India. New Delhi, PPH, 1973.

Hasani, Syed A. Hai
India during the Muslim rule. Lucknow, Academy of Islamic Research & Publication, 1977.

Hossain, Hameeda
Company weavers of Bengal: The East India Company and the organisation of textile production in Bengal, 1750-1813. Oxford: OUP, 1983.

Iqbal, Afzal
Life and times of Mohammad Ali: An analysis of the hopes, fears and aspirations of Muslim India from 1778-1931. Delhi, Idara-i-Adabiyat-i-Delhi, 1978. (rpt)

Ishwari Prasad
India in the eighteenth century. Allahabad, Chugh Pub. 1973

Jaffer, S.M.
Some cultural aspects of Muslim rule in India. Delhi, Idarah-i-Adabiyat-i-Delhi, 1972.

Jain, B.S.
Glimpses of Indian traditions. Delhi, D.K. Publishers, Distributors, 1988.

Jain, Purushottam C.
Socio-economic exploration of Medieval India from 800 to 1300. A.D. Delhi, B.R.Pub., 1976.

Kabir, A.M.Fazle
Libraries of Bengal, 1700-1947: The story of Bengali Renaissance. London, Mansell, 1987.

Kejariwal, O.P.
Asiatic Society of Bengal and the discovery of India's past, 1784-1838. Oxford: OUP, 1988.

Lelyveld, D.
Aligarh's First generation: Muslim solidarity in British India. New Delhi, OUP, 1978.

Major, Richard H. ed.
India in the 15th century. (n.p), B. Franklin, 1970. (Hakhuyt Society Series, 22)

Majumdar, R.C.
History and culture of Indian people. V.6. Delhi Sultante. (1300-1526 A.D.). Bombay, Bharatiya Vidya Bhavan, 1980.

History and Culture of the Indian people. V.7. Mughal Empire. (1526-1707 A.D.) Bombay, Bharatiya Vidya Bhavan, 1974.

Manuoci, Niccolao
Storia de Mogol or Mogul India, 1653-1708. Tr. with introduction and notes by William Irvine. 5.v.in 4. New Delhi, Oriental, 1891.

Mukherjee, S.N.
Sir William Jones: A study of eighteenth century British attitudes to India. New Delhi, Orient Longman, 1987.

Medieval Indian culture. Aga, Shivlal Agarwal, 1970.

Narain, Vishnu Anugrah
Social history of modern India: Nineteenth century. Meerut, Meenakshi, Prakashan, 1972.

Naqvi, Hamida K
Agricultural, industrial and urban dynamism under the Sultans of Delhi, 1206-1555. New Delhi, Munshiram Manoharlal, 1986

Nizami K.A.
Politics and society during the early medieval period: Collected works of Prof. Muhammed Habib. New Delhi, PPH, 1982.

Ojha, P N
Aspects of medieval Indian society and culture. New Delhi, Classic, 1978.

North Indian social life during the Mughal period. Delhi, Oriental Publishers and Distributors, 1975.

Orme, Robert
Of the Govt. and people of Hindustan:Extracts from the authors work entitled historical fragments of the Mughal Empire. Lucknow, Pustak Kendra, 1971.

N. CULTURE

N. a. Historical Role

Ahsanullah, M.
History of the Islamic World. New Delhi, Deep & Deep, 1986

Ali, B. Shaik
Islam: A cultural Orientation. New Delhi, Macmillan, 1981

Ali, K
Study of Islamic History. Delhi, Idara-i-Adabiyat-i-Delhi, 1980

Amini, M Taqi
Reconstruction of Culture in Islam. Tr. by Z.A. Usmani, New Delhi, Kitab Bhavan, 1988

Ali, Syed Ameer
Amir Ali on Islam: Essays on Islamic history and culture and his historical letters to the Time from 1891-1928. Ed. Imtiaz Ali. Delhi, Amar Prakashan, 1982

Islamic history and culture. Delhi, Amar Prakasham, 1981 (rpt)

Short History of the Saracens. New Delhi, Kitab Bhavan, 1981 (rpt)

Ashraf, K. Mohammad
Life and condition of the people of Hindustan, 1200-1550 A.D. New Delhi, Munshiram Manoharlal, 1870

Asiatic Society, Calcutta.
Proceedings of the Asiatic Society Comp. and Ed. by Sibadas Chandhuri, v.1. Calcutta, 1980

Askari, Syed H
Aspects of the cultural history of Medieval Bihar. Patna, K.P. Jayswal Research Institute, 1984

Banerjee, Anil C.
State and society in Northern India, 1206-1526. Calcutta, K.P. Bagchi 1982.

Bartol, d.
Mussulman culture Tr. from Russian by Shahid Suhrawardy. Philadephia, Porcupine Press, 1977 (Studies in Islamic History, no.3) (original Russian published by Calcutta Univ., 1934).

Bhargava, K.D.
Survey of Islamic culture and institution. Allahabad, Kitab Mahal, 1981.

Chirol, Velentine.
India: A historical survey of political, economic and intellectual developments. New Delhi, Deep and Deep, 1983.

Enam, M. Abdulla
Decisive moments in the history of Islam. New Deli, Idara-i-Adabiyat-i- Delhi, 1984.

Fidai, R.A.
Concise history of Muslim World. Tr. New Delhi, Kitab Bhavan, 1988.

Gulati, S.P.
Quintessence of Islamic history and culture. Delhi, Amer Prakashan, 1986.

Hasan, Amir
Palace culture of Lucknow. Delhi: B.R.Pub. Corp., 1983.

Hosain, Saiyid Safdar.
Early history of Islam. 2V. Delhi, Inter India, 1985.

History of the Muslims of Indo-Pakistan sub-continent (1707-1806) Vol.1 Lahore: Research society of Pakistan 1978, (Publ. Research Soc. Pakistan, 52)

History of Mughal India: A detailed study of political, economic, social and cultural aspects from 1526 to 1707 AD. Delhi, Surjeet, 1984.

Iqbal, Afzal
Culture of Islam: The classical period. Lahore, Inst. of Islamic Culture, 1974.

Israel, M. & N.K. Wagle. Ed.
Islamic Society and Culture: Essays in honour of Professor Aziz Ahmed. Delhi, Manohar, 1983.

Srivastava, Muta Prasad
Social life under the Great Mughals, 1526-1700 A.D. Allahabad: Chugh Pubns., 1978

Sahu, Kishori Prasad
Some aspects of North Indian social life, 1000-1526 A.D. (with special reference to contemporary literatures). Calcutta, Punthi Pustak, 1973.

Sarkar, Jadunath
Study of eighteen century India. Calcutta, Saraswar Library, 1976.

Thoughts of trends of cultural contacts in medieval India. Calcutta: OPS Publishers, 1986.

Sarkar, Jagdish N
Mughal Economy: Organisation and working, Calcutta, Naya Prakash, 1987.
Survey of research in social and economic history of India. Delhi, Ajanta, 1986.

Srivastava, Musta Prasad
Society and culture in the medieval India. 1206-1707 Allahabad, Chugh, 1975

Sufi, G.M.D.
Islamic Culture in Kashmir. New Delhi, Light & Life Publishers, 1979.

Suhrawardy, Shahid
Cultural history of the Muslims. New Delhi, Mittal, 1986.

Verma, H.C.
Dynamics of urban life in pre-Mughal India. New Delhi, Munshiram Manoharlal, 1986

Yusuf, S.M.
Studies in Islamic history and culture. Delhi, Adam Pubs, 1986.

N.b. Salient Features

Ali, Syed Amir
Spirit of Islam: A History of the Evolution and Ideals of Islam with a Life of the Prophet. Delhi, Idara-i-Adabiyati-i-Delhi, 1978.

Haneef, Susanne
What everyone should known about Islam and Muslims. Delhi, Taj Co., 1986.

Hanifi, M.Jamil
Islam and the transformation of culture. Bombay Asia, 1974.

Mahmudun-Nasir, S.
Islam: Its concepts and History. New Delhi, Kitab Bhavan, 1984.

Nadwi, Abul Hassan A.
Islam and civilization. Lucknown, Acad, 1985.

Religion and civilization. Lucknow, Acad, 1980.

Pickthall, Muhammad Marmaduke.
Cultural side of Islam. Ed.3. New Delhi, Kitab Bhavan, 1981, (rpt.)

Qadir, Abdul M.
Studies in Islamic socio-economic thought. Hyderabad, Inst. Indo-Mid. East Culture Studies, 1975.

N.C. Indo-Islamic Dimensions

Ahmad, Aziz.
Intellectual history of Islamic India. Edinburgh, Scotland. Edinburgh Univ. Press, 1970.

Muslim self-statement in India and Pakistan, 1857-1968. New York, International Pub. Services, 1970.

Grover, Satish.
Architecture of India-Islamic (727-1707 A.D.). New Delhi, Vikas, 1981.

Holt, P.M.
Cambridge History of Islam. vol.2 part a Indian subcontinent, ... Massachusets, Cambridge Univ. Press, 1977-78.

Islamic Heritage of India.
New Delhi, National Museum, 1986.

Jones, L.B
People of the Mosque. Delhi, C.L.S., 1980

Kausar, Ali
Study of Islamic history. Calcutta, Mullick Bros., 1971

Khan, Y.S
Glimpses on Medieval Indian culture. Bombay, Asia, 1970

Khuda Bakhsh, Salahuddin
Arab civilization. Delhi, Idara-i-Adabiyat-i-Delhi, 1980

History of Islamic people. Delhi, Idara-i-Adabiyat-i-Delhi, 1983.
Islamic civilization. 2v. Calcutta, Calcutta University, 1970.

Orient under the caliphs. Delhi, Idara-i-Adabiyat-i-Delhi, 1984

Studies: Indian and Islamic. Delhi-,Idarah-i-Ababiyati-i-Delhi, 1978.

Mujeeb, Muhammad
Islamic influence on Indian society. Meerut, Meenakshi, 1972.
World history: Our heritage, Bomaby, Asia, 1970

May, L.S.
Evolution of Indo-Muslim thought from 1857 to the present. New Delhi (Distr. D.K. Publishers), 1988.

Nath, R.
Islamic architecture and culture in India. Delhi, B.R. Publications, 1983.

Roy, M Nath
Historical role of Islam. Lahore: Sind Sagar Academy, 1974

Saba'I, Mustafa
Some glittering aspects of the Islamic civilization. Tr. by Sharif Ahmad Khan. Delhi, Hindustan, 1983

Sarkar, Jagdish N
Islam in Bengal. Calcutta, Ratna Pyblications, 1975

Savory, R,M.
Introduction to Islamic civilization New Delhi, Vikas, 1980

Siddiqi, I.H.
Islam and Muslims in South Asia: Historical perspective. Delhi,

Adam Pub., 1986

Stepaniants, M.T.
Islamic philosophy & social thought (in 19th &.20th centuries). Lahore, People's Publishing House, 1989

Schimmel, Annemarie
Islam in the Indian subcontinent. Leiden, Brill, 1980.

Sharif, Jafar
Islam in India. Ed. William crooke. New Delhi, Arnold Heineman, 1975.

Singh, Attar, ed.
Socio-cultural impact of Islam on India. Chandigarh, Punjab Univ. Publications Bureau, 1976.

Tarachand
Influence of Islam on Indian culture. (Second edition.) Allahabad: The Indian Press (Publications) Private Ltd. 1976.

N.d. Art
N.d.a. General

Chandra, Jagdish
Bibliography of Indian arts, history and archaeology. (Dr. Anank K. Coomaraswamy memorial volume. Vol. 1: Indian art.). Delhi: Delhi Printers Prakashan, 1978.

Craven, Roy C.
A concise history of Indian art. London: Thames & Hudson, 1976. (Includes Islamic India: architecture and painting.)

Desai, Ziyauddin
Mosques of India. New Delhi, Publications Division, Ministry of Information and Broadcasting, 1971.

Farooqi, Anis
Arts of India and Persia. New Delhi. D.K. Publishers Distributors, 1979.

Fehervari, G. & Y.H. Safdari
1400 years of Islamic art: A descriptive catalogue. London, Khalili Gallery, 1981.

Harie, J.C.
Art and Architecture of the Indian Subcontinent. London, Penguin, 1986.

Mehta, Rustam J.
Masterpieces of Indo-Islamic architecture. Bombay: Taraporevala, 1976.

Michell, George. e.d.
Islamic heritage of Bengal: Protection of the cultural heritage. Lanham, Unipub., 1984. (Research papers no.1).

Nath, R.
Historigraphical study on Indo-Muslim architecture: Medieval architecture of India and Pakistan. Jaipur: Historical Research Documentation Programme, 1989.

Jharokha: An illustrated glossary of Indo-Muslim architecture. Jaipur: Historical Research Documentation Programme, 1986.

Rahman, Syed Mustafizur
Islamic caligraphy in Medieval India. Dhaka: University Pr., 1979.

Roy, Asim.
The Islamic syncretistic tradition in Bengal. Princetion: Princetion University Press, 1983.

Shokoohy, Mehrdad.
Bhadreswar: A study on the oldest Islamic monuments in India. Leiden, Brill, 1987.

Salar Jung Museum
Journeys in Art through the Salar Jung Museum. Hyderabad, Salar Jung Museum Board, 1971.

s

Saraf, D.N.
Arts and crafts, Jammu and Kashmir: Land, people and culture. New Delhi, Abhinav Publications, 1987.

N.d.b. Pre-Mughal

Hasan, Syed Mahmudul.
Mosque Architecture of pre-Mughal Bengal. (2 rev.ed.) Dhaka Univ. Pr., 1979.

History of Sultanate architecture. New Delhi, Abhinav Pub., 1978.

N.d.c. Mughal

Brookes, John.
Gardens of Paradise: The history and design of the Great Islamic gardnes. London: Weidenfeld & Nicholson, 1987.

Clark, C. Stanley
Moghul Art and Architecture. New Delhi, Metropolitan Book Co. (Distributor), 1988.

Colnaghi, P & D.
Persian and Mughal art. (Exhibition catalogue.) London: 1976.

Hambly, Gavin
Cities of Mughal India. (Delhi, Agra and Fatehpur Sikri.) New Delhi: Vikas, 1977.

Nath, R.
Architecture of Fatehpur Sikri: Forms techniques and concepts. Jaipur: Historical Research Documentation Programme, 1988.

Calligraphic art in Mughal architecture. Jaipur, Historical Reasearch Decumentation Programme, 1985

Colour decoration in Mughal archietecture: India and Pakistan. 2nd rev. ed. Jaipur, Historical Research Documentation

Programme, 1989.

History of decorative art in Mughal architecture. Delhi, Motilal Banarsidas, 1976
History of Mughal architecture. 5 vols. Jaipur, Historical Research Documentation Programme, 1986

Immortal Taj Mahal
Jaipur, Historical Research Documentation Programme, 1975

Some aspects of Mughal architecture. New Delhi: Abhinav Pubns., 1976.

Taj Mahal and its incarration: Original Persian date on its builders, material, coats measurements. etc. Jaipur: Historical Research Documentation Programme, 1985.

Parihar, Subhash
Mughal monuments in the Punjab and Haryana. New Delhi, IIP. 1985.

Shokoohy, Mehrdad and N.H. Shokoohy
Hisar-i-Firuza: Sultanate and early Mughal architecture in the District of Hisar, India, (Monograph on Art, Archaeology and Architecture.) London (n.p.), 1988.

Smart, E. and D.S. Walker
Pride of the Princes: Indian arts of the Mughal Era in the Art-Mughal Cincinnati Art Museum. Cincinnati, Ohio: Cincinnati Art Museum, 1986.

Titley, Norah M
Plants and gardens in Persian, Turkish and Mughal art. London: The British Library, 1979.

Verma, Som Prakash
Art and material culture in the paintings of Akbar's court. New Delhi: Vikas, 1978.

N.d.d. Post-Mughal

Ames, Frank
Kashmir shawl and Its Indo-French influence. Woodbridge, Suffolk: Antique Collectors Club, 1986.

Davies, P
Splendours of the Raj: British architecture in India, 1660-1947. London, Murray, 1985.

Levi-Strauss, Monique
Cashmere shawl. London: Dryal Press, 1987.

Michell, George
Islamic Heritage of the Deccan. Bombay, Marg Publications, 1986.

Nayeem, M.A.
Splendour of Hyderabad: Last phase of an Oriental Culture, 1591-1948 A.D. Bombay, Jaico, 1987.

Qureshi, M.R.
Wajid Ali Shah's theatrical genius. New Delhi, Metropolitan Book, Co., 1987.

N.d.e. *Painting*

Atil, Esin.
The Brush of the masters: drawings from Iran and India. Washington: Freer Gallery of Art, 1978.

Beach, Milo Cleveland.
Early Mughal painting (Polsky Lectures). Cambridge, Harvard Univ. Press. 1988.

The grand Mogul: Imperial painting in India. 1600-1660 Williamstown, Mass: Sterling & Francine Clark Art Inst., 1978.

Brijbhushan, Jamila
The world of Indian miniatures. Tokyo: Kodansha International, 1979.

Bussagli, Mario
Indian miniatures. (Transl. by Raymond Rudoff from the Italian original). New Delhi: Macmillan 1976.

Chandra, Pramod and Deniel J. Ehnbom
The Cleveland, Tuti-nama manuscript and the origins of Mughal painting. Cleveland, Museum of Art. 1976.

Clarke, C. Stanelay.
Mughal paintings: The School of Jahangir. New Delhi, Motilal Banarsidass, 1983.

Comaraswami, Anand K.
Mughal paintings. New Delhi, Indological BK House, 1982.

Mughal painting: Catalogue of the Indian collections in the Museum of Fine Arts, Boston. Delhi, Bharatiya Pub., House, 1981.

Das, Asok Kumar.
Mughal paintings during Jahangir's time. Calcutta: Asiatic Society, 1981.

Splendour of Mughal Painting. Bombay, Vikas, 1986.

Falk, Toby.
Indian paintings, Mughal and Rajput and a Sultanate manuscript. London: P. & D. Colnaghi, 1978.

Hingorani, R.P.
Painting in South Asia: a bibliography. Varanasi: Bharatiya Pubishing House, 1976.

Paintings from the Muslim courts of India. An exhibition held in the Prints and Drawings Gallery, British Museum, 13 April to 11 July 1976, (Compiled by R.H. Pinder-Wilson with the assistance of E. Smart and D. Barrett) London: World of Islam Festival Publishing Co. 1976.

Titley, Norah M.
Miniatures from Persian Manuscripts. A catalogue and subject

index of paintings from Persia, India and Turkey in the British Library and the British Museum. London British Museum Publication Ltd. for British Library. 1977.
Persian Painting, fourteenth century. New Delhi: Arnold Heineman Publishers, 1977.

Sports and pastimes: Scenes from Turkish, Persian and Mughal paintings. London: British Library, 1969.

Welch, Stuart Cary.
Imperial Mughal painting. London, Chatto & Windus, 1978.

N.e Military Strategy

Roy, Atual Chandra
Mughal Navy and Navel Warfare. Calcutta, World Press, 1973.

Sensarma P.
The military history of Bengal. Calcutta: Naya Prokash. 1977.

Zaman, Mohammed Khaiser
Mughal artillery. Delhi, Idarah-i Adabiyal-i Delhi, 1983. IAD Orientl (Original) Series, 22)

N.f Sciences

Afaq, S.H. and M.M.H. Siddiqui
Pharmacognosy, phytochemistry, pharmacology and clinical studies of Unani Medicinal Plants. V. 1. Aligarh, A.K. Tibbiya College, Aligarh Muslim University, 1984.

Bag, A.K.
Mathematics in ancient and medieval India. Varanasi. Chaukhamba Orientalia, 1979.

Hussaini, M. Mazhar
Food and nurtition in Islam. New Delhi, Kitab Bhavan, 1981.

Jaggi, O.P.
Science and techology in medieval India. Delhi, Atma Ram,

1977.

Kabir, Humayun
Science, democracy, & Islam: And other Essays. (n.p), AMS Press, 1977

Khan, M.A. Rahman
Muslim contribution to science and culture. Delhi, Idarah-i-Adabiyat-i-Delhi, 1980.

Khan, Majid Ali
Islam on origin and evolution of life. Delhi, Idara-i-Adabiyat-i-Delhi, 1979.

Khuda Bukhsh,
Contributions to the history of Islamic civilization Lahore. Accurate Printers, 1975.

Mahmud, Syed Jafar
Metal technology in medieval India. New Delhi. D.K. Publishers Distributors, 1988.

Mitchiners, Micheal.
Oriental coins and their values. Non-Islamic states and western colonies, A.D. 600-1979. Sanderstead: Hawkins Publs, 1979 (Include Afghanistan, the Ghaznawids, the coming of Islam to Northern India, Islamic Sultanates of Malaya and Indonesia).

Nadvi, K.S.
Darwinism on trial. Durban, Islamic Medical Association, 1986.

Nasr, S. Hossein
Islamic science: An illustrated study. Brooklyn, Interlink Pub. 1976.

Western science and Asian cultures. New Delhi, Indian Council for Cultural Relations, 1976.

Qaisar, Ahsan Jan
Indian response to European technology and culture, A.D. 1498-1707. Delhi, Oxford Univ. Press, 1982.

Rahman, A.
Science and technology in medieval India: A bibliography of source materials in Sanskrit, Arabic and Persian. New Delhi, Indian National Science Academy, 1982.

Said, Hakim Mohammad
Pharmacy and medicine through the ages. Karachi, Hamdard Foundation, 1980.

Siddiqui, A. Hameed
Critical look at the theory of evolution. Delhi, Crescent Pub. Co., 1984.

P. BIOGRAPHY

Pa. General

Ahmad, Fazl
Five heroes of Islam. Delhi, Kutub Khana Ishayat-ul-Islam, 1978.

Ahmed Kh. J.
Hundred great Muslims. Chicago, Kazi, Pub. 1975

Beale, T.W.
Oriental Biographical dictionary. Rev. enl. ed. by H. George Keene, Ludhiana, Kalyani, 1972.

Eminent Mussalmans. New Delhi, Neeraj Pub. House, 1981.

Eman, M.A.
Ibn Khaldun: His life and works. New Delhi, Kitab Bhavan, 1984.

Fidai, R. A.
Companions of the holy Prophet, 2. V. New Delhi, Adam 1986.

Hasan, M.
Historians of Medieval India. Meerut, Meenakshi, 1989.

Hussain, M. Hadi
Imam Abu Hanifa: Life and Work. New Delhi, Kitab Bhawan, 1988.

Hussain, S. Athar
Glorious Caliphate. Lucknow, Academy of Islamic Research and Publication, 1974.

Jain, Naresh Kumar
Biographical Dictionary of Muslims in the Indian sub-continent, 1957-1976. Columbia, South Asia Books, 1978.

Muslims in India: A Biographical Dictionary. V.2 (K-z) New Delhi, Manohar Publications, 1983.

Muslims in India: A Biographical Dictioanry. V1. (A-J) New Delhi, Manohar Publications, 1980.

Kalia, D.R. and M.K. Jain
Eminent Indians: A bibliography of bibliographies. New Delhi, Marwah Publications, 1977.

Keene, H.G.
Oriental Biographical Dictionary. New Delhi, Manohar Reprint, 1971.

Moin, Mumtaz
Umm al-Mu 'minin' A' ishah Siddiquah: life and work. Delhi, Taj, 1982.

Nadvi, Abdul Hassan A.
Islam and the earliest Muslims. Lucknow, Academy of Islamic Research, 1985.

Nadvi, Sayyid Sulaiman
Hadhrat Ayesha Siddiqa: Her life and works. Tr. Syed Athar Husain. Kuwait, Islamic Book Publishers, 1986

Nomani, Shibli
Al-Farooq: Life of Umar the Great, second Caliph of Islam New

Delhi, Adam Pub. 1986.

Qadir, Abdul
Famous Urdu Poets and Writers. ed.2 New Delhi, Seemant Prakashan, 1977.

Saxena, Ram Babu
European and Indo-European poets of Urdu and Persian. Jaipur, Historical Research Documentation Programme, (Distributor), 1985

Sharma, J.S.
National Biographical Dictionary of India. New Delhi, sterling, 1972.

Pb Medieval India
Pba Miscellany

Abbas, F. Zareen
Abdul Qadir Badauni: As a Man and Historiographer. Delhi, Idara-i-Adabiyat-Delhi, 1987.

Bayley, Emily
The golden calm: An English lady's life in Moghul Delhi: Reminiscenes, ed, by M.A. Kaye. Exeter: Webb & Bower; 1980.

Fox, Ralph.
Chenghis Khan. Dehra Dun, English Bk Depot, 1975.

Dutta. M. A.
Siraj-ud-Daula. New Delhi, Oriental Longman, 1971.

Godden, Rumer.
Gulbadan: Portrait of a rose princess at the Mughal court. London, Macmillan Press, 1980.

Jhangiani, S.M.
Shah Abdul Latif and his Times, 1690-1751 A.D. Delhi, University of Delhi, 1987.

Khan A Saeed, Comp.
Bibliography of the works of Abul Raihan al Biruni. New Delhi, INSA. 1982.

Khan, I. Alam
Political biography of a Mughal Noble Munim Khan: Khan-i-Khanan. New Delhi, Oriental Pubs. 1973.

Nizami, Khaliq Ahmed
Life and times of Shaikh Farid-ud-din Ganj-i-Shakr. Delhi, Idara-i-Adabiyat-i-Delhi, 197

Pant, Chandra
Nur Jahan and her family. Allahabad: Dandewal, 1978.

Quamr-ud-din, M.
Life and times of Prince Murad Baksh. Delhi, (n.p.), 1974.

Rai, Lakhpat
Sarmad: His life and rubais. Gorakhpur, H.P.P. Samarak Samiti, 1978.

Said, Muhammad and Ansar Zaid Khan
Al-Biruni: His times, life and works. Jaipur, Historical Research Documentation Programme (Distributor) 1981.

Sarkar, Jagdish Narayan
Life of Mir Jumla: The General of Aurangzeb. New Delhi, Rajesh Publications, 1979.

Sethi, V.K.
Kabir: The weaver of God's name. New Delhi, Manohar, 1986.

Singh, Gurmit
Guru Nanak's relationship with the Lodis and the Mughals. New Delhi, Atlantic, 1987.

Tanaskar, B.G.
The life and work of Malik Ambar. Delhi, Idarah-i Adabiyat-i Delhi, 1978.

P.b. Abul Fazal (d. 1608)

Alavi, Azra
Socio-religious out-look of Abul Fazl. Delhi, Idara i-Adabiyat-i-Delhi, 1984.

Pbc Hazrath Khwaja Moinuddin Chishti (d. 1236)

Begg, W.D.
Holy biography of Hazrat Khwaja Muinuddin Chishti. London, East-West-Pub. 1978.

Currie, P.W.
Shrine and cult of Muinal-Din Chisti of Ajmer. New Delhi, OUP, 1989.

P.b.d. Mohammad Dara Shikuh (d. 1659)

Hasrat, Bikrama. J
Dara Shikuh: Life and works. New Delhi, Munshiram Manoharlal, 1982.

P.b.e. Hazrath Amir Khusru Dehlawi (d.1325)

Ansari, Zoe, ed.
Life and times of Amir Khusraw Dehlevi. New Delhi, S. Chand and Co. 1980.

Amir Khusrau
Seventh Centenary celebrations 11th -13th February, 1972. Hyderabad, Abul Kalam Azad Oriental Research Institute, 1976.

Rahman, A.S. Sabahuddin
Amir Khusru as a genius. Delhi, Idara-i-Adabiyat-i-Delhi, 1982.

P.b.f Shah Waliyullah Dehlawi (d. 1766)

Baljon, J.M.E.

Religion and thought of Shah Wali Allah Dihlawi, 1703-1762. Lerden, Brill, 1986.

Jalbani, G.N. Ed.
Teachings of Hazrat Shah Waliyullah Muhaddis Dehlvi. New Delhi, Kitab Bhavan, 1988.

Muztar, A.D.
Shah Wali Allah, A saint scholar of India. Islamabad: National Institute of Historical & Cultural Research, 1979.

Rizvi, Saiyid Athar Abbas.
Shah Wali-Allah and his times: A study of eighteenth century, Islam, politics, and society in India. Canberra: Ma'rifat P.H. 1980.

P.c Builders of Modern India
P.c.a Miscellany

Abbas, Khwaja Ahmed
Bombay, My Bombay: Love story of the City. New Delhi, Ajanta, 1987.

Abul Kalam Azad Oriental Research Institute (Hyderabad).
Ali Yavar Jung Commemoration Volume. Bombay, Popular Prakashan, 1983.

Ahmed, Mohiuddin
Saiyd Ahmed Shaheed. Lacknow, Academy of Islamic Research & Publications 1975.

Ahmad, Qeyamuddin and J.S. Jha
Mazharul Haque. New Delhi, Govt. Press, 1976. (Builders of Modern India).

Ahmad, Riaz
Jinnah and Jauhar: Points of contact and divergence. Islamabad: Quaid-i-Azam University, 1979.

Ahuja, N.D.

Khatun-e-Ajam: Quarrat-ul-Ayn. Delhi, Harnam, 1984.

Aziz, K.K.
Complete Works (1933-1947) of Rahmat Ali. Islambad: National Institute of Historical & Cultural Research, 1978.

Ali, S. Akbar, ed.
Nawab Mehdi Nawaz Jung Memorial Volume. Hyderabad, Maulana Abul Kam Azad Oriental Research Institute, 1970.

Ali, Syed Ameer
Memories and Other Writings. Ed. Syed Razi Wasli. Delhi, Renaissance Pub. House, 1985.

Andrews, Charles Freer
Zaka Ullah of Delhi. Lahore, University Books, 1976.

Dwivedi, A.N.L.
Syed Amanuddin: His mind and art. New Delhi, Sterling, 1988.

Hamid, Khwaja A.
An Autobiography. Bombay, Lalvani, 1972.

Jalal, Ayesha
Sole spokesman: Jinnah, the Muslim League and the demand for Pakistan. Cambridge, Oxford University, Press, 1985.

Khuda Bakhsh, Salahuddin and Jadunath Sarkar
Khuda Bakhsh: A biography of the founder of the Khuda Bakhsh Library. Patna, Khuda, Bakhsh Oriental Public Library, 1981.

Kidwai, M. Hashmi
Rafi Ahmed Kidwai: Builders of Modern India. New Delhi, Publications Division, 1986.

Kumar, I.
Mir Taqi Mir. Delhi: Sahitya Akademi, 1982.

Merriam, A.H.

Gandhi & Jinnah. Columbia, South Asia Bks. 1980.

Moazzam, Anwar
Jamaal-Din-al-Afghani: A Muslim intellectual. New Delhi, Concept, 1984.

Murad, Mehr Afroz
Intellectual modernism of Shibli Nu'mani: An exposition of his religious and socio-political ideas. Foreword by Charles J. Adams. Lahore: Institute of Islamic Culture, 1976.

Nadwi, Abul Hasan A.
Life & mission of Maulana Mohammed Ilyas. Lucknow, Academy of Islamic Research 1983.

Pant, Sudhir
Asaf Ali: Patriot & humanist. New Delhi, NBT, 1984.

Qadiri, Khalid H.
Hasrat Mohani. Delhi, Idara-i-Adasiyati-i-Delhi 1985.

Rehmaney, F.A. Aziz
My Eleven years with Fakhruddin Ali Ahmed. New Delhi, S.Chand, 1979.

Ram Malik. ed.
Hakeem Abdul Hameed: Felicitation. New Delhi, Vikas, 1983.

Hali. Delhi: Sahitya Akademi, 1982.

Shaikh, M. Hajjan
Maulana Ubaid Allah Sindhi: A revolutionary scholar. Islamabad: National Institute of Historical & Cultural Research. 1986.

Swayne - Thomas. A.
Indian summer: a Memsahib in India and Sind. London. New English Library, 1981.

Saiyid, Matlubul Hasan
Political study of Mohammad Ali Jinah. Vol. I & II. Delhi, Anmol Publication, 1966.

Tirmizi, S.A.I. ed.
Autobiography of Lutfullah: An Indian's perceptions of the West. New Delhi, Interantional Writers, 1986.

Tytler, Harriet
An English women in India: The Memoirs of Harriet Tytler, 1828-1858. Oxford, Oxford Univ. Press, 1986.

P.c.b *Sheikh Muhammad Abdullah (1905 - 1982)*

Abdullah, Sheikh M.
Autobiography. New Delhi, Vision Books, 1983.

Sheikh Mohammad Abdullah's views explained. Srinagar, J & K. State People's Convention, 1970.

Kaul, R.N.
Sheikh Mohammad Abdullah: A political pheonix. New Delhi, Sterling, 1985.

Taseer, C. Bilqees
Kashmir of Sheikh Mohammad Abduallah. Lahore, Ferozson, 1986.

P.c.c *Maulana Mohammad Ali (1878-1931)*

Ahmed, Khwaja M. ed.
Maulana Muhamad Ali Centenary Volume. Hyderabad, Abul Kalam Azad Oriental Research Institute, 1978

Akhter, Rafiqe. ed.
Historical trial: Maulana Mohammad Ali and Others. Karachi, East and West Pub. co. 1971.

Hasan, Mushir-ul.
Mohammed Ali: Ideology and Politics. New Delhi, Manohar Publications, 1981.

Mohammed Ali in Indian politics: Select writings 2V. New Delhi, Atlantic Publications, 1982.

Mohammad Ali
My Life a Fragment: An Autobiographical Sketch of Maulana Muhammed Ali. Iqbal, Afzal. Ed. Delhi, Seema Pub. 1979.

Select writings and speeches of Maulana Muhammad Ali (new ed). 2 vols. Lahore: Islamic Book Foundation, 1987.

P.c.d *Maulana Abul Kalam Azad (d. 1958)*

Abduhu, G. Rasool
Educational Ideas of Maulana Abul-Kalam Azad. New Delhi, Sterling, 1975.

Aiyer, Subramania R.
Role of Maulana Abul Kalam Azad in the Indian politics: Hyderabad, Abul Kalam Azad Oriental Research Institute, 1984.

Azad A. Kalam
Indian wins freedom: An autobiographical narrative. New Delhi, Orient Longman, 1988.

Douglas, Ian H.
Abul Kalam Azad: An intellectual, religious biography. New Delhi, D.K. Publishers & Distributors 1988.

Gandhi, Rajmohan
India wins errors: A scrutiny of Maulana Azad's India wins freedom. New Delhi, Gian, 1989.

Nizami, Khaliq Ahmed
Maulana Azad Album (Urdu with English translation). New Delhi, D.K. Publishers Distributors, 1988.

Siddiqi M. Murtaza
Religious philosophy of Maulana Azad. Hyderabad, Abul Kalam Azad Oriental Research Institute, 1985.

P.c.e *Mirza Asadullah Khan Ghalib (1797-1869)*

Ghalib Academy (New Delhi)
Ghalib Bibliography. New Delhi, 1970.

Kumar, Ish,
Ghalib and Iqbal Chandigarh: Panjab Univ. Publications, Bureau, 1988.

Mahmud, Sayyid Fayyaz,
Gahlib: A Critical Introduction. Jaipur, Historical Research Documentation Programme (Distributor) 197

Ram, Malik,
Mirza Ghalib. 2nd ed. New Delhi; National Book Trust, 1980.

Saran, Saraswati
Mirza Ghalib, the poet of poets. New Delhi, Munshiram Manoharlal Pub, 1976.

P.e.f ***Dr. Zakir Hussain (d. 1969)***

Mathur, V.S. ed.
Zakir Hussain: Educationalist & teacher. New Delhi, Arya Book Depot, 1970.

Mujeeb, M.
Dr. Zakir Hussain: Delhi, NBT, 1972.

Noorani, A.G.
President Zakir Hussain. Delhi, Hind Pocket Books, 1970.

Singh, Dayanita
Zakir Hussain: A photo essay. New Delhi, Himalayan, 1987.

Zakir Hussain: A symbol of Indian Democracy. New Delhi, Publications Division, 1970.

P.e.g. ***Allama Sir Muhammad Iqbal (d. 1938)***

Akbar-Ali, Sheikh
Iqbal: His poetry and message. New Delhi, Deep & Deep Pub, 1988.

Ansari, Asloob Ahmad ed.
Iqbal: Essays and studies. New Delhi, Ghalib Academy, 1978.

Ashraf. S. Ahsan
Critical exposition of Iqbal's philosophy. Patna, Book Associated Agency, 1978.

Azhar, Malik Mueen Nawaz
A Bibliography of articles on Iqbal (1900-1977). Lahore, Islamic Book Service, 1978.

Bashir, Javed Kamran
Iqbal And secular nationalism (post-1908 phase). Lahore, Progressive Publishers, 1977. (Progressive series, 41).

Burney, S.M.H.
Iqbal: Poet-patriot of India. New Delhi, Vikas, 1987.

Haq, Q. M. and M.I Waley,
Allama Sir Muhammad Iqbal: Poet-philosopher of the East. London, British Museum Publications, 1977.

Hasan, Ahmad S.
Iqbal: His political Ideas at Crose roads. Aligrah, Printwell Pub. 1980.

Hasan, Masud-ul
Life of Iqbal. Book 1. Lahore, Ferozsons (1978).

Hussain, Riaz
Iqbal poet and his politics. New Delhi, Uppal House, 1987.

The politics of Iqbal: A study of his political thought and actions. Lahore, Islamic Book Sercie, 1977.

Iqbal, Sir Muhammed
Life, art and thought. Proceedings of the Iqbal Centenary Symposium. University of Ottawa, 1977; ed. by L. Librande, N. Yar Khan. Ottawa, Canada-Pakistan Association, 1979.

Jafri, Ali Sardar and K.S. Duggal. ed.
Iqbal commemorative volume. New Delhi: All India Iqbal Centenary Celebrations Committe, 1980.

Khan, Asif Iqbal
Some aspects of Iqbal's thought. Lahore, Islamic Book Service, 1977.

Malik, Ghulam Rasool
Iqbal and the English romantics. New Delhi, Metropolitan Book Co. (Distributor), 1988.

Maruf, Mohammad, ed.
Contributions to Iqbal's thought. Lahore, Islamic Book Service, 1977.

Iqbal's philosophy of religion: A study in the congnitive value of religious experience. Lahore, Islamic Book Service. 1977.

Nadvi, S. Abul Hasan Ali
The glory of Iqbal. Translated by M.A. Kidwai (rev. ed.). Lucknow, Academy of Islamic Research and Publication, 1979, (Its: Publication series, no. 71).

Nuruddin, Abu Sayeed
Allama Iqbal's attitude towards Sufism and his unique philosophy of Khudi (self). Dacca, Islamic Foundation Bangladesh, 1978.

Rashid, Khawaja Abdul
Iqbal, Quran and the western world. Lahore, Progressive Books. 1978.

Rastogi, T.C.
Western Influence in Iqbal. New Delhi, Ashish, 1987.

Rizvi, Syed Jamil Ahmad
Theses on Iqbal. A bibliographical survey of the theses on Iqbal sumbitted to the University of the Punjab, Lahore, 1950-1976. Lahore, Aziz, 1977.

Siddiqui, Misbah-ul-Haq
Iqbal: A Critical Study. Lahore, Farhan Publishers, 1977.

Siddiqui, Nazeer
Iqbal and Radhakrishnan: A comparative study. New Delhi, Sterling, 1989.

Singh, Kushwant
Muhammed Iqbal. New Delhi, OUP, 1982.

Usmani, Muh. Adil and Nasim Fatima
Books on Allama Iqbal in university libraries of Pakistan: Allama Iqbal birth centenary celebrations. 1977. Karachi: University, 1977. (Karachi: University Library publications).

P.c.h *Sir Syed Ahmed Khan* (1817-1898)

Aligarh Muslim University: Maulana Azad Library
Sir Syed Ahmed Khan: A Select Bibliography. Aligarh, 1971.

Dar, Bashir Ahmed
Religious thought of Sayyid Ahmed Khan. 2nd-ed. (n.p) 1971.

Graham, G.F.I.
Life and work of Syed Ahmed Khan. Delhi, Idara-i-Adabiyat-i-Dilli, 1974.

Hali, Altaf Hussain
Hayat-e-Javed: A biography of Sir Syed Ahmed Khan. Trans. by K.H. Qadiri & D.J. Mattews. Idara-i-Adabiyat-e-Dilli, 1979.

Hussain, M. Hadi
Syed Ahmed Khan. Lahore, Institute of Islamic culture, 1970.

Malik, Hafiz
Sir Syed Ahmed Khan's educational philosophy: A documentary records. Islamabad, National Institute of Historical & Cultural Research, 1989.

Political profile of Sir Syed Ahmad Khan. Islamabad, National Institute of Historical & Cultural Research, 1981.

Sir Syed Ahmad's institution building activities: A documentary profile. Islamabad, National Institute of Historical & Cultural Research, 1989.

Sir Syed Ahmad Khan and Muslim modernization in India and Pakistan. New York, Columbia U. Press, 1980.

Muhammad, Shan
Sir Syed Ahmed Khan: A political bigoraphy. Meerut, Meenakshi, 1970.

Successors of Sir Syed Ahmed Khan. Delhi, Idara-i-Adabiyat-i-Delhi, 1981.

Writings and Speeches of Sir Syed Ahmad Khan. Bombay, Nachiketa, 1972.

Nizami, Kaliq A.
Sir Syed Album. Delhi, Idarah-i-Adabiyat-i-Delhi, 1984.

Sayyid Ahmad Khan: Bibliography. New Delhi, Publications Division, 1974.

Troll, Christian Wilhelm
Sayyid Ahmad Khan: A reinterpretation of Muslim theology. Delhi, Vikas Pub. House, 1978.

P.c.j. *Justice Badruddin Tayabji (1844-1906)*

Noorani, A.G.
Badruddin Tayabji. New Delhi, Publication Division, 1971.

Shakir, Moin
Muslims and Indian National Congress: Badruddin Tayabji and his times. Delhi, Ajanta Pub. 1987.

Q. UMMAH

Q.a. Demography

Lal, K.S
Growth of Muslim population in medieval India, 1000-1800 A.D. Delhi, Research Publication in Social Sciences, 1973.

Shaikh, A H.
Socio-economic and political testament of 100 million Indian Muslims. Bombay, (n.p.), 1978.

Siddiqui, Nafis A.
Population geography of Muslims of India. Delhi, S. Chand, 1976.

Q.b. Muslims as Minority

Communist Party of India
Muslim minority and the Communist Party. New Delhi, Communist Party of India, 1975.

Ghosh, S.K.
Protection of minorities and Schedule Castes. New Delhi, Ashish, 1984.

Haskar, U.
Minority protection and international Bill of Human Rights. New Delhi, Allied, 1974.

Imam, Muhammad.
Minorities and the law. Bombay, N.M. Tripathi, 1972.

Islam, M. Nurul.
Bengali Muslim public opinion as reflected in the Bengali Press, 1901—1930. Dacca, Bangla Academy, 1973.

Kettani, M.A.
Muslim minorities in the world today. London, Mansell, 1986.

Kumar, A.
Cultural and educational rights of the minorities under Indian constitution. Delhi, Deep and Deep, 1986.

Lahiri, D.K. & B.J. Dev
Assam Muslims: Politics cohesion. Delhi, Mittal, 1985.

Madan, T.N.
Muslim communities of South Asia: Culture and society. New Delhi, Vikas, 1976.

Meerza, Delawar H.A.
Muslim modernism in Bengal: Selected writings. Dacca, Dacca Univ. Press, 1980.

Misra V.B.
Evolution of the constitutional history of India (1773-1947) with special reference to the role of the Indian Congress and the minorities. New Delhi, Metropolitan Book Co. (Distributor), 1987.

Motamar al-Alam al-Islami
Country by country outline survey of Muslim minorities of the world. Karachi, 1977.

Rakkar, J.S.
Muslim politics in the Punjab. New Delhi, Deep & Deep, 1985.

Shakir, Moin
Politics and minorities. Delhi, Ajanta Pub. 1980.

Sharma, Jagdish N.
India's minorities: A bibliographical study. New Delhi, Vikas, 1975.

Srinivasan, N.
Identity crisis of Muslim: Profiles of Lucknow youth. New Delhi, Concept, 1981.

Srivastava, G.N.
Language controversy and the minorities. Delhi, Atma Ram,

1970.

Wadhwa, K. Kumar
Minority safeguards in India. Delhi, Thompson Press, 1975.

Zaidi, Abdul Momin
Congress and the minorities: Preserving national cohesion; A study of Congress polity towards minorities during the last 100 years. Delhi, Indian Inst. Applied Political Res., 1984.

Q.c. *Family*

Ahmed, Imtiaz
Family, kinship and marriage among Muslims in India. New Delhi, Manohar Book Service, 1976.

Begum, H. H. Jahan
Muslim married couple. New Delhi, Award Pub. House, 1982.

Ilahi, M.A.
Polygamy. Bombay, Inst. of Islamic Studies, 1970.

Lessons to learn by married couples. Tr. From Urdu and Gujarati. Karachi, Peermahomed Ebrahim Trust, 1976.

Q.d. *Sociological Perspectives*

Ahmed, Rafiuddin
The Bengal Muslims, 1871-1906: A Quest for identity. Delhi, OUP. 1981.

Ahmed, Sufia
Muslim community in Bengal, 1884-1912. Dacca, OUP. 1974.

Ali, Abdullah Yusuf
Life and labour of the people of India. New Delhi, Inter India Pub. 1986.

Ali, Hashim Amir
The Meos of Mewat: Old neighbours of New Delhi. Oxford-IBH.

1970.

Ali, M. Hasan
Observations on the Musulmans of India, descriptive of their manners, customs, habits and religious opinions, 2 v. New Delhi, Idara-i-Adabiyat-i-Delhi, 1973.

Battye, Evelyn
Costumes and characters of the British Raj. New Delhi, Roli Bks, 1982.

Bhagi, M. L.
Medieval India: Culture and thought. Ambala Canntt. The Indian Pub, 1974.

Engineer, Asghar A.
Muslim communities of Gujarat. Bombay, Institute of Islamic Studies, 1989.

George, Alexandra.
Social ferment in India. London, Athlone Press, 1986.

Khan, M. Huq.
Social pathology of the Muslim society. Delhi, Amar Prakashan, 1978.

Khan, Mumtaz A.
Mass conversions of Meenakshipuram: A Sociological Enquiry. Madras, C.L.S. 1983.

Mishra, S.C.
Muslim communities in Gujarat: Preliminary studies in their history & social organisation. New Delhi, Munshiram Manoharlal, 1985.

Naqvi, Hameeda K.
Urbanisation & urban centres under the Great Mughals. Delhi, Orient Book Dist. 1971.

Parpola, A & B.S. Hansen ed.

South Asian religion and society. New Delhi, D.K. Publishers Distributors. 1986.

Qureshi, Ishtiaq H.
Muslim community of the Indo-Pakistan subcontinent, 610 - 1947: A brief historical analysis. Delhi, Renaissance, 1985.

Roy, Shibani and S. M.H. Rizvi
Muslims: Bio-cultural perspectives. New Delhi, B.R. Publishing Corporation, 1984.

Shamsuddin.
Meos of India: Their custom and laws. New Delhi, Deep and Deep Pub. 1987.

Smith, W.C.
Modern Islam in India: A social analysis. New York, Russell & Russell, 1972.

Q.e *Social Contract*

Ahmed, Ilyas
The Social contract and the Islamic state. New Delhi, Kitch Bhavan, 1981.

Q.f. *Social Structure*

Aggarwal, P.C.
Caste, religion & power: An Indian Muslim case. New Delhi, Shri Ram Centre Industrial Relations, 1971.

Ahmed, Akbar S.
Pakistan society: Islam, ethmicity and leadership in South Asia. Karachi, OUP 1987.

Ahmad, Imtiyaz.
Caste and social stratification among the Muslims. New Delhi, Manohar Book Service, 1973.

Ali, Ashraf.
Muslim Elite. New Delhi, Allantic Publishers, 1980.

Maddison, Angus.
Class structure & economic growth: India & Pakistan since the Moghuls. (n.p) Norton, 1972.

Oman, J.C.
Brahmans, theists & Muslims of India. Delhi, Orient Bk. Dist. 1973.

Rizvi, S.A. Abbas
Religious and intellectual history of the Muslims in Akbar's reign 1556-1605 with special reference to Abul Fazal. New Delhi, Munshiram Manoharlal, 1975.

Santha, K S
Begums of Awadh. Varanasi, Bharati Prakashan, 1980.

Siddiqui, Iqtidar H.
Mughal relations with Indian ruling elite. New Delhi, MRML, 1983.

Singh, Harjinder. ed.
Caste among non-Hindus in India. New Delhi, National Pub. House, 1978.

Spear, Percival
Nabobs: A study of the social life of the English in 18th century India. London, Curzon Press, 1982.

Yalland, Zoe.
Traders and Nabobs: The British in Cawnpore, 1765-1857. Salisbury, Russell, 1988.

Q.g. *Shias*

Rizvi, S.A. Abbas
Shias in India. 2v. New Delhi, Munshiram Manoharlal, 1986.

Hasnain, Nadam
Shias and Shia Islam in India: A study of society and culture.

New Delhi, Metropolitan Book Co. (Distributor), 1988.

Hollister, O.N.
Islam and Shia's faith in India. Delhi, Amar Prakasham, 1988.

Hussain, Abdul
Gulzara Daudi for the Bohras of India: A short note on the Bohras of India, their 21 Imams and 51 Dais with their customs and tenets. Surat, The Author, 1977.

Husain, Abrar S.
Marriage customs among Muslims in India: A sociological study of Shia marriage customs. New Delhi, Sterling, 1976.

Nanji, Azim
Nazari Ismaili tradition in the Indo-Pakistan Sub-continent. Delmar, New York, Caravan Books, 1978.

Nomani, M. Manzoor
Khomeni, Iranian revolution and the Shite faith. London: Al furqan Publications, 1988.

Q.h. ***Social Change***

Ahmad, Imtiaz
Modernisation and social change among Muslims in India. Columbia, South Asia Books, 1982.

Khan, Mumtaz A.
Muslims in the process of rural development in India. New Delhi, Uppal, 1984.

Kumedan, B.S.
Modernisation and social reforms among the Muslims: A select bibliography. Delhi, Delhi School of Social Work, 1978.

Nadvi, Syed Abul Hasan Ali.
Basis of a new social order. Lucknow, Academy of Islamic Research and Publications, 1977.

Q.i. *Revivalism*

Abbasi, M.Y.
Genesis of Muslim fundamentalism in British India. New Delhi, Metropolitan Book Co. (Distributor), 1987.

Agwani, M.S.
Islamic fundamentalism in India. New Delhi, Twenty First Century, 1987.

Ahmed, Tariq
Raushaniya movement. Delhi, Idarah-i-Adabiyat-i-Delhi, 1983.

Religio-political forment in the N.W. Frontier during the Mughal Period: The Raushaniya movement. Delhi, Idarah-i-Adabiyat-i-Delhi, 1982.

Alam, M. Manzoor.
Islamic movement: Intellectual and practical dynamism. Delhi, Crescent Pub. Co., 1982.

Message of Islam and approaches of dai. Delhi, Crescent Pub. Co., 1984.

Role of Muslim youth in reconstruction of contemporary world. Delhi, Crescent Pub. Co. 1983.

Ashraf, Mujeeb
Muslim attitudes towards British rule and western culture in India. Delhi, Idara-i-Adabiyat-i-Delhi, 1982.

Ayub, Mohammed
Politics of Islamic reassertion. New Delhi: Vikas, 1982.

Aziz, K.K.
Indian Khilafat Movement 1915-1933: A documentary record. Karachi, Pak. Publishers, 1972.

Bakshi, Fasihuddin
Wahabi movement. New Delhi, Classical Pub. Co., 1983.

Bakshi, S.R.
Gandhi and Khilafat. New Delhi, Gitanjali, 1985.

Bamford, P.C.
History of the Khilafat & non-cooperation movements. New Delhi, K.K. Book Distributors, 1985 (rpt.).

Bjorkman, J. ed.
Fundamentalism, revivalists and violence in South Asia. Delhi, Manohar, 1988.

Bondarevsky, C.
Muslims in the west. New Delhi, Sterling, 1983.

Engineer, Asghar A.
Islam and revolution. Delhi, Ajanta Books Int., 1984.

Ghazali, Imam
Ihya ul-alumuddin. al Tr. Fazlulkarim. 4v. New Delhi, Taj Co. 1986.

Haq, Syed Moinul
Islamic thought and movements in the subcontinent. 711-1947, Karachi Pakistan Historical Society, 1979. (Pakistan Historical Society Pulication, no. 69).

Iqbal, Sir Muhammed
Reconstruction of religious thought in Islam. 3rd ed. New Delhi, Kitan Bhavan, 1984.

Kaviraj, N.
Wahabi and Faraizi rebels of Bengal. New Delhi, People's Pub. House, 1982.

Mez, Adam
Renaissance of Islam. Tr. By Khuda Baksh and D.S. Margoliouth. New Delhi, Kitab Bhavan, 1979.

Minault, Gail

Khilafat movement: Religious symbolism and political mobilisation in India. New Delhi, Oxford Univ. Press, 1982.

Mutahhari, Murtaza
Islamic movements in the twentieth century: Translated by Maktab-e Quran. Kashmir, India. (2nd ed.) Tehran, Great Islamic Library, 1979.

Nadvi, S.Habibul Haq
Islamic resurgent movement in the Indo-Pak subcontinent: A critical analysis of the 18th and 19th centureis. Durban, Academia, 1987.

Niemeger, A.C.
Khilafat movement in India, 1919-1929. Netherland (n.p.) 1972.

Qamaruddin
Mahdavi movement in India. Delhi, Idara-i-Adabiyat Delhi, 1985.

Rashid, M. Abdur
Islam in the Indo-Pakistan subcontinent: An analytical study of the Islamic movements. Lahore, National Book Foundation, 1977.

Rizvi, S.A. Abbas
Shah Abd al' Aziz: Puritanism, sectarian, polemic and jihad. New Delhi, Munshiram Manoharlal, 1982.

Smith, Donald E.
Religion and political modernisation. (includes an essay on Indian ulama and the Khilafat movement). New Haven, Yale Univ. Press, 1974.

Tiwari, J.G.
Islamic fundamentalism in Asia. Aligarh, Humanist Publications, 1987.

Zakaria, Rafiq
Rise of Muslims in Indian politics: An Analysis of development from 1885-1906. Bombay, Somaiya Pub., 1970.

Q.k. *Muslim Organizations.*

Abbasi, M. Yusuf
First Muslim political organisation of British India: A documentary record. Islamabad, National Institute of Historical and Cultural Research, 1989.
History of London Muslim League. 1908-1928. Islamabad, National Institute of Historical and cultural Research, 1989.

Abdulla, Ummi
Malabar Muslim Company. New Delhi, Orient Longman, 1981.

Aziz, K.K.
All India Muslim Conference 1928-1935: A Documentary Record. Karachi, National Pub. House, 1972.

Bahadur, K.P.
History of London Muslim League: 1908-928. Islamabad,, National Institute of Historical and Cultural Research, 1989.

Engineer, Asghar Ali
Bohras. New Delhi. Vikas, 1980

Hyder, Ghulam
Politics of Jamat-e-Islami-e-Hind. New Delhi, CPI, 1974.

Poonawala, Ismail, K.
Bibliography of Ismaili literature. Malibu, Undena Pub., 1977.

Rahman, M.
From Consultation to confrontation: A study of the Muslim League in British Indian politics, 1906-1912. New York, State Mutual BK., 1985.

Rizvi, S.A. Abbas
Socio-intellectual History of the Isna Ashri Shis in India. New Delhi, Munshiram Manoharlal, 1986.

Roy, Shibani
Dawoodi Bohras: An Anthropological perspective. Delhi, B.R.

Publishing Corporation, 1985.

Sadiq, Naqvi
Qutb Shahi Ashur Khanas of Hyderabad city. Hyderabad, Babul-Ilm Society, 1982.

Shakir, Moin
Theory and practice of Jammat-e-Islami (Hind). New Delhi, Sampradayikta Virodhi Committee, 1978

Wasey, Akhtar-ul.
Education of Indian Muslims: A study of the All India Muslim Educational Conference (1886-1947). New Delhi, Press Asia Inst., 1977.

R. CONTEMPORARY ISSUES

R.a *Babri Masjid and other Monuments*

Ahmed, Nilofaur & R.L. Shfukla
Babri Mosque or Rama Janam Temple. New Delhi, Institute of objective Studies, 1986.

Husain, Ashraf
Record of all the Puranic and Non-Historical Epigraphs on the Protected Monuments in the Delhi Province. New Delhi, Manager of Publications. 1987.

Shukla, R. L and Ahmad, N.
Babri Mosque. New Delhi, Crescent, 1986.

R.b *Communalism*

Afaque, Khan M.
Gandhian approach to communal harmony: A critical study. Delhi, Ajanta Publications, 1986.

Ansari, Iqbal A.
Study in communal relations: the Muslim relation in India. New Delhi, Metropolitan Book Co. (Distributor), 1988
Ahmedabad. riots: Focus on dark corners. Delhi, Radiance Book

Depot, 1970.

Ayde, S. Rao
Communal riots in India: A legal, sociological politcal study. New Delhi, sampradayikta Virodhi Samiti, 1972.

Chandra, Bipan
Communalism in Modern India. 2nd ed. New Delhi, Vikas, 1988.

Engineer, Asghar Ali
Bhiwandi - Bombay Riots: Analysis & documentation. Bombay, Inst. of Islamic Studies, 1985.

Communal riots in the post-independence India. Hyderabad, Sangam Books, 1984.

Communalism and communal violence in India. New Delhi,. Gian, 1989.

Delhi Meerut Riots. Delhi, Ajanta, 1987.

Ethnic Conflict in South Asia. Delhi. Ajanta, 1987.

Ghosh, S.K.
Communal riots in India. New Delhi, Metropolitan Book Co. (Distributor), 1987.

Joshi, S.
Is RSS behind communal riots? New Delhi, Sampradayikta Virodhi Committee, 1975.

Kashyap, Anirban
Communalism & constitution. New Delhi, Lancer, 1988.

Noorani, A.G.
How does riot begin & spread? New Delhi, sampradayikta Virodhi Committee (S V.C) 1970.

Ranchi riots: Inquiry Committee Report x-rayed. New Delhi S.V.C., 1970.

Rajgopal, P.R.
Communal Violence in India. New Delhi, Uppal, 1987.

Sinha, K and Lutfi, Q
Bibliography on communal (Hindu, Muslim) tensions (pilot fasciules). New Delhi, Documentation Centre, Gandhi Peace Foundation, 1970.

Thursby, G.R.
Hindu-Muslim relation in British India: A study of controversy, conflict and communal movements in Northern India, 1923-28. Londen-Brill 1975.

Vakil, A.K.
Three dimensions of Hindu-Muslim confrontation. Calcutta, Minerva, 1981.

R.c *Family Planning*

Khan, M.E.
Family planning among Muslims in India: A study of the reproductive setting. New Delhi, Manohar Publication, 1979.

Mahmood, Tahir
Family planning in the Muslim viewpoint. New Delhi, Vikas, 1984.

Rd *India Today*

Ahmad, S. Maqbol
Indo Arab Relations. New Delhi, ICCR, 1978.

Allapicha, A.M.
Just a peep into the Muslim mind. Madras (n.p.) 1973.

Ansari, Iqbal A.
Muslim situation in India. New Delhi, Sterling, 1989.

Baig, M.R.A.
Muslim dilemma in India. New Delhi, Vikas, 1974.

Baldev
India, Pakistan & Muslim politics. New Delhi, International Report, Pub., 1976.

Ballhatchet, K & D. Taylor ed.
Changing South Asia. 5 Vols. Hongkong, Asian Research Service, 1989.

Banerjee, Brejendra Nath
Religious conversions in India. New Delhi, Harnam Pub. 1982.

Barnabas, Manorma ed.
Challenge of societies in transition. Delhi, Macmillan, 1976.

Bedar, Abid R.
Problem of reforms among Indian Muslims. (n.p.) Kohinoor, 1970.

Bhattacharya, S. and R. Thapar
Situating Indian history for Sarvepally Gopal. New Delhi, OUP 1986.

Blackham, R.J.
Incomparable India: Tradition, supersitition, Truth. London, Sampson, 1981.

Borden, C.M. ed.
Contemporary India: Essays on the cases of tradition. Delhi, O.U.P., 1989.

Carre, Anwar
Islam and the state in the world today. New Delhi, Manohar, 1987.

Coward, Harold G.
Modern Indian responses to religious pluralism. New York, State Univ. of New York. Press, 1987.

Dalwai, Hamid Umar
Muslim politics in secular India. Delhi, Hind Pocket Books, 1973.

Muslim politics in India. Bombay, Nachiketa, 1970.

De Amalendu
Islam in modern India. Calcutta, Maya Prakashan, 1982.

Engineer, Asghar Ali
Islam and Muslims: A critical reassessment. Jaipur, Printwell, 1985.

Islam-Muslims-India. Bombay, Look Vangmaya Griba, 197.

Gandhi, Rajmohan
Understanding the Muslim mind. London. Penguin, 1988.

Gauba, K. Latif
Passive voices: A penetrating study of Muslims in India. New Delhi, sterling, 1973.

Gaur, Raj Bahadur
Glorious Telangana armed struggle. New Delhi, CPI, 1973.

Ghosh, S.K.
Muslim politics in India. New Delhi, Ashish, 1987.

Muslims in India Democracy. Delhi, Ashish, 1983.

Hamid, Muhammad
Unholy alliance: Indo-Israel collaboration against the Muslim world. Lahore, Islamic Book Centre, 1978.

Hamid, Saiyid
Problems of Indian Muslims. Patna, Khuda Bakhash, Oriental Public Library, 1985.

Huq, Manzoorul
Muslims in India. New Delhi, Publication Division, 1985.

Haq, Mushiul
Islam in India's transition to modernity. Bombay, Orient Longman, 1979.

Muslim politics in modern India. Meerut, Meenakshi, 1970.

Harman, S.
Plight of Muslims in India. New Delhi, D.K. Publishers, 1976.

Hasan, Qamar
Muslims in India: Attitudes, adjustments, and reaction. New Delhi, Northern Book Centre, 1987.

Hussain, S. Showkath
Human rights in Islam. New Delhi, Kitab Bhawan, 1988.

Imam, Zafar. ed.
Muslims in India. New Delhi, Orient Longman, 1975.

Jain, Sushila
Muslims & Modernization. Jaipur, Rawat Pub. 1986.

Khan, Ehsanullah
Characteristics and behaviour of nations (India in turmoil). New Delhi, Bait at Hikmah Trust, 1988.

Khan, S.G. Hossein
Seir mutaqherin: or review of modern times in 4 vols. (1923-1931). New Delhi, D.K. Publishers Distributor, 1982.

Khurshid, Salman
At home in India. A reassessment of Indian Muslims. New Delhi, Vikas, 1986.

Lokhandwalla, S.T. ed.
India and contemporary Islam. Simla, Indian Institute of Advanced Study, 1971.

Maamiry, Ahmad Hamoud
Islamism and economic prosperity in Third World countries. New Delhi, Lancers, 1983.

Madhok. B.
Punjab problem: the Muslim connection. Delhi, Hindu World Publications, 1985.

Mathur, V.B.
Muslims and changing India. New Delhi, Trimurti Publications, 1972.

Moazzam, Anwar ed.
Islam and contemporary Muslim World. New Delhi, Light and Life Publishers, 1981.

Mujeeb, Muhammed
Indian Muslims. New Delhi, Munshiram Manoharlal, 1985.

Nadvi, Abul Hassan A.
Fifteenth Century. Lucknow, Academy of 1972

Islam & the world. Tr. from Arabic by Mohammed Kidwai. Kuwait, IIFSO, 1977.

Muslims in India Tr. from Urdu by Mohd. Asif Kidwai, Lucknow, Academy of Islamic Research & Publication, 1976.

Mussalman. Tr. from Urdu by Moniuddin Ahmed. Lucknow, Academy of Islamic Research & Publications, 1972.

Reconstruction of Indian society-What Muslims can do. Lucknow, Academy of Islamic Research, 1972.

Western civilization: Islam & Muslims. Tr. from Urdu by Mohd-Asif Kidwai. Lucknow, Academy of Islamic Research Publications, 1974.

Nath, R.
Historical questions, controversies and anomalies. Jaipur, Historical Research Documentation Programme, 1989.

Pavier, Berry
Telangana movement, 1914-1951. New Delhi, Vikas, 1981.

Prasad, Yuvaraj Deva
Indian Muslims & World War I: A phase of disillusionment with British rule; 1914-1918. New Delhi, Janaki Prakashan, 1985.

Rao, D.V.
Telangana armed struggle and the path of Indian revolution: A critique of Telangana people's struggle and its lessons. Ed. 2 Hyderabad, Proletarian Line pub, 1982.

Rashid, Sh. Abdur
Perspectives on South Asia: Select articles. Islamabad, National Institute of Historical and Cultural Research, 1989.

Rastogi, Tara Chand
Muslim World: Islam breaks fresh ground. New Delhi, Ashish, 1986.

Reddy, Arutla Ramachandra
Telangana struggle memoirs, New Delhi, PPH. 1985.

Schimmel, Annemarie
From Sanai to Maulana and Iqbal. Kabul, University of Kabul, 1977.

Shakir, Moin
Muslim attitude: A trend report and bibliography. Aurangabad, Parimal Prakashan, 1974.

Muslims in free India New Delhi, Kalamkar Prakashan, 1972.

State and politics in contemporary India. Delhi, Ajanta Pub. 1986.

Smith, W.C.
Modern Islam in India. New Delhi, Manohar, 1979.

Stevenson-Hamilton. V.E.O.
Yes, Your Excellency. London: Harmsworth, 1985. (Reminiscences of north-west India, 1934-47).

Swarup, Devendra

Politics of conversion. New Delhi, Deen Dayal Research Inst., 1986.

Thanawi, Ashraf Ali
Answer to modernism, by Ashraf Ali Thanwi, translated by M.H. Askari and Karrar Husain. Karachi, Maktaba Daruloom 1976.

Troll, Chirstian W
Islam in India: Studies and commentaries. v.3.: The Islamic experience in contemporary thought. Delhi, Chanakya Publications, 1986.

Tyabji, Badruddin
Reflection on the completion of the 1400 years of the Hejri calendar: The Hindu Muslim syndrome, Islam & the modern world (problems & prospects). Patna, Khada Bakhsh Oriental Public Libram, 1981.

Vahiduddin, S.
Muslim thought in a changing world: Islam and modern challenges, Islam; problems & prospects. Patna, Khuda Bakhsh Oriental Public Libran, 1982.

William, R.B.
Religions of immigrants from India and Pakistan: New thread in American tapestry. Cambridge, Cambridge Univ. Press, 1988.

Zakaria, Rafiq
Rise of Muslims in Indian politics, Ed. 2. Bombay, Somaiya, 1971.

Zwemer, W.B.
Mohammendan world of today. Allahabad, Chaugh Publications, 1976.

S. WOMEN

S.a Women's Socio-religious Status

Baveja, Malik Ram
Women in Islam. (Tr. of 'Awart Islami talim'). Hyderabad, Institute of Indo-Middle East Cultural Studies, 1988 (rpt).

Engineer, Asghar Ali
Status of women in Islam. Delhi, Ajanta, 1987.

Hali, K.A. Hussain
Voices of Silence: English translation of khwaja Altaf Hussain Hali's Majalis-un-Nissa and Chup-Ki-Dad, by Gail Minault. Delhi, Chanakya Publication, 1986.

Jung, Anees
Unveilling India: A women's journey. New Delhi. D.K. Publisher Distributors, 1987.

Khan, M. Huq
Purdah and polygamy: A Social pathology of Muslim society. New Delhi, Harnam Publications, 1981.

Mahmood, Tahir
Grandeur of womehood in Islam. Lucknow, Academy of Islamic Research & Publications, 1977.

Menon, M. Indu
Status of Muslim women in India: A case study of Kerala. New Delhi, Uppal Publishing House, 1981.

Mernissi, Fatima
Women in Muslim paradise. New Delhi, (N.P.) 1986.

Minault, Gail
Extended family: Women and political participation in India and Pakistan. Delhi, Chanakya Publications, 1981.

Nadvi, Abul Hassan
Status of women in Islam. Lucknow, Academy of Islamic Research, 1975.

Papanak, H and Gail Minault, ed.

Seperate worlds: Studies of Purdah in South Asia. New Delhi, Chanakya Publications, 1982.

Rizvi, Parveen.
Is purdah a hindrance to progress. Tr. by Syed Iqbal Zaheer. Bangalore, Pioneer's Association, 1977.

Roy, Shibani
Status of muslim women in North India. Delhi, B.R. Publishing Corporation, 1979.

Sharma, Arvind
Women in world religions. Albany, State University of New York Press, 1986.

Siddiqui, M.S.
Blessed Women of Islam. Delhi, Islamic Book Trust, 1983.

Siddiqi, M.Iqbal
Islam forbids: Free mixing of men and women. Delhi, Adam Publications, 1986.

Subbamma, Malladi
Islam and Women. New Delhi, 1988.

S.b. Women Today

Baxamusa, Ramala
Muslim women of Bombay: Bombay, Research Unit on Women's Studies, Vithaldas Vidya Vihar, SNDT Women's University 1984.

Brijbhushan, Jamila
Muslim women in purdah and out of it. New Delhi, Vikas, 1981.

Chauhan, Indira
Purdah to profession: A case study of working women in M.P. New Delhi, D.K. Publishers, Distributors, 1986.

De Souza, A.
Women in contemporary India and South Asia. New Delhi, Manohar, 1980.

Jain, Devak, ed.
Indian Women. New Delhi, Publications Division, Ministry of Information and Broadcasting, 1975.

Nanda, B.R. Ed.
Indian Women: From purdah to modernity. New Delhi,: Vikas, 1976.

Siddiqui, H.Y.
Muslim women in transition: A social profile. New Delhi, Harnam, 1987.

S.c. Women - Yesteryears

Cooper, Elizabeth
Harim and the purdah: Studies of oriental women. Delhi, Bimla Pub. House, 1983. (rpt.)

Lal, K.S.
Mughal harem. New Delhi, Aditya Prakashan, 1988.

Mukherjee, I.L.A
Social status of North Indian women, 1526-1707 A.D. Agra, Shiva Lal Agarwala, 1972.

Simharay, Diana.
Warring women of India: Lives of Rani Jhansi, Zebun-Nisa, daughter of Aurahgzeb; Tarabai; Bahinabai and Mira. Bombay, Colour Publications, 1973.

Tirmizi, S.A.I.
Edicts from the Mughal harem. Delhi, Idara-Adabiyat-i-Delhi, 1979.

Young, K.K. and Arvind Sharma
Images of feminine-mythic, philosophic and human in the

Buddhist, Hindu and Islamic traditions: A bibliography of women in India. Chico, Calif., New Horizons Press, 1974.

S.d. Women studies - Guide to Resources.

Azmat, Tahera
Women mentors of men. (Biographical sketches of ten women). Ujjain, Siddharatha Prakashan, 1970.

Cour, Ajeet and Arpana Cour, ed.
Directory of Indian women today, 1976. New Delhi, India International Publications, 1976.

Dasgupta, Kalpana
Women in the Indian scene: An annotated bibliography. New Delhi, Abhinav Publications, 1976.

Hasan, Masud-ul-
Daughters of Islam: Being short biographical sketches of 82 famous Muslim Women (including 20 relevant to South Asia.). Lahore, Hazrat Data Ganj Bakhsh Academy, 1976.

Kabir, Kausar and Inamul Kabir
Biographical dictionary of prominent Muslim ladies. New Delhi, Light and Life Publishers, 1983.

Lytle, Elizabeth
Women in India: A comprehensive bibliography. Monticello, 11., Vance Bibliographies, 1978.

Naji, Ghulamali Ismail.
Guidance for women. Tr. from Urdu and Gujarati. Karachi, Peermahomed Ibrahim Trust, 1973.

S.N.D.T. University, Bombay Research Unit on Women Studies.
Select bibliography on women in India. Bombay, Allied Publishers, 1975.

Sakala, Caroel
Women of South Asia: A guide to resources. Millwood, N.Y.

Kraus International, 1980.

Vashishta, B.K. ed.
Encyclopaedia of Indian Women, 1976. New Delhi, Praveen Encyclopeadia Publications, 1976.

Who's Who of Indian Women, International.
Madras, National Biographical Centre, 1977.

T. INFORMATION SOURCES: A SELECT LIST.

Abidi, Sartaj, A. and S.K. Sharma
Fifty Years of Indian History Writings. Index Articles in Journal of Indian History. V.1 — 50 (1921/22 - 1972). New Delhi, Gitanjali Prakashan, 1974.

Abu Dawud,
Sunan Abu Dawaud. 3v. Delhi, Al-Madina, 1986.

Abu Dawud
Sunan Tr. and Notes by Ahmed Hasan. New Delhi, Kitab Bhavan, 1987.

Abul-Fazl, Mirza
Sayings of the Prophet Muhammed. New Delhi, Award Pub. House, 1977.

Ahmed, Jamiluddin, Comp:
Historic Documents of Muslim freedom movements. Lahore, United Pub., 1970.

Ahmad, Qayamuddin
Corpus of Arabic and Persian inscriptions of Bihar, A.D. 640-1200. Patna, K.P. Jayaswal Research Inst., 1973.

Ali, A. Yusuf.
Holy Quran: Text, Translation and commentary. New Delhi, Kitab Bhavan, 1982.

Meaning of the Illustrious Quran (Being a textless edition of the

English Trnaslation of Holy Quran by Allama Abdullah Yusuf Ali). New Delhi, Kitab Bhavan, 1978.

Ali, Ahmed.
Al-Quran: A Contemporary Translation, New Delhi. OUP, 1987.

Ali, Rahman
Islamic architecture in India: After independence; A review reasearch. Bull. Deccan Coll. Res. Institute. 37: 1-4 (1977-1978), 107-117.

Ali, S. Ashfaq
Guide to Bhopal: A research Publication with Illustrations depicting a socio-cultural scene of Bhopal with special reference to the gas tragedy of Bhopal. Bhopal, Jai Bharat Pub. House, 1987.

Aligarh Muslim University. Maulana Azad Library.
Sir Syed Ahmed Khan, A Select Bibliography. Aligarh, 1971.

American Institute of Indian Studies.
Primary sources for 16th-19th century studies in Bengal, Orissa and Bihar Libraries. Ed. Katharine S. Delhi. Culcutta, 1971.

Andhra Pradesh, State Archieves.
Mughal archives: A descriptive catalogue of the documents pertaining to the reign of Shah Jahan, 1628-1658. Hyderabad, 1977. V.1.

Mughal documents: Catalogue of Aurangazeb's reign. Ed. and Comp. by M.A. Nayeem. V.1. Pt. 1, Hyderabad, 1980.

Aneesuddin, Mir
Index to the Holy Quran. Hyderabad, Islamic Academy of Sciences, 1988.

Ansari, Shahabuddin.
"Islam and Islamic Studies: An Annual bibliography of articles", Islam and the Modern Age, 13 (1982) 252-303; 14 (299-303); 15(1984), 209-300; 17 (1986), 33-131; 22 (1989), 43-150.

Ashraf, Muhammad
A concise descriptive catalogue of the Arabic manuscripts in the Salar Jung Museum & Library. Volume IV: Concerning 448 manuscripts of Islamic Theology (Shiite). Hyderabad, Salar Jung Museum & Library, 1981 (Salar Jung Museum & Library Publications, New Series 10/4)

Ashfaq, Ahmed And Ahmed Saeed Khan
Religion: A bibliography. Aligarh, Centre of West Asian Studies and Institute of Islamic Studies, 1970.

Asiatic Society, Calcutta.
Asiatic Researches, Comprising History and Antiquities, the Arts, Science and Literature of Asia. 24 V., New Delhi, Cosmo, 1979.

Catalogue of Arabic Manuscripts in Tabular Form. Prepared by K.M. Maitra. Rev. and ed. by M.S. Khan. Calcutta, 1980.

Ayyangar, S. Krishnaswami, Ed.
Sources of Vijayanagar History. Delhi, Gian Pub. House, 1986.

Aziz, A. Muhammad
Political History and Institutions of the Early Turkish Empire of Delhi, 1206-1290 A.D. New Delhi, Oriental Books Reprint Corp. 1972.

Aziz, K.K.
All India Muslim Conference, 1928-1935. A Documentary Record. Karachi, National Pub. House, 1972.

Indian Khilafat Movement, 1915-1933: A Documentary record. Karachi, Pak Publishers, 1972.

Muslims under Congress rule, 1937-1939. A Documentary record. 2V. Delhi, Renaissance Pub. House, 1986.

Azmat, Tahera
Women mentors of men. (Biographical sketches of ten women). Ujjain, Siddharatha Prakashan, 1970.

Bagvi, Malik B.A.,
Learner's guide to the division of inheritance. New Delhi, Kitab Bhavan, 1981.

Beale T.W.
Oriental biographical dictionary. Rev. enl. ed. by H. George Keene. Ludhiana, Kalyani, 1972.

Bhattacherje, S.B.
Encyclopaedia of Indian dates and events, New Delhi, Sterling, 1987.

"Bibliography of Quranic Studies", Islam and the Modern Age. 9:3, (Aug. 1978), 92-102.

Binark, I. and H. Eren
World bibliography of translations of the meanings of the Holy Quran: Printed translations, 1515-1980. London, Keagen Paul International, 1987.

Bukhari, Imam
Shahi al-Bukhari, V.5. Translated with Notes by Mohammed Asad. New Delhi, Kitab Bhavan, 1978.

Sahih al-Bukhari Translation of the meanings, by M. Mushin Khan. 9 Vols. New Delhi, Kitab Bhavan, 1980.

Chandra, Jagdish
Bibliography of Indian art, history & archaeology (Dr. Anand K. Coomaraswamy memorial volume. Vol.1: Indian Art.) Delhi, Delhi Printers Prakashan, 1978.

Chatterjee, A.
Indian reference publication: A bibliography. Calcutta, Mukherjee Book House, 1974.

Cheema, Pervaiz I.
Select Bibliography of periodical literature on Indian and Pakistan, 1947-70. 3V. Islamabad, National Institute of Historical & Cultural Research. 1984.

Coomaraswamy, A.K.
Mughal painting: Catalogue of the Indian collections in the Museum of Fine Arts, Boston. Delhi, Bharatiya Pub. House, 1981.

Cour, Ajeet & Arpana Cour. ed.
Directory of Indian women today, 1976. New Delhi, Indian International Publications, 1976.

Cutchi Memon Jamat of Andhra Pradesh.
Directory of Members. Secunderabad, 1986.

Dadarkar, Ahmed Bahauddin
Daily prayer book of Islam. Bombay, Taj Publishers, 1987.

Dalvi, Muhammad Abdur - Rahim
1400 years of Islam: A desk-book. Pune, Muhammad Dalvi Wakf, 1989.

Daryabadi, A. Majid.
Tafsir-ul-Quran 4V. Lucknow, Academy of Islamic Research and publications, 1981-1985.

Dasgupta, Kalpana
Women on the Indian Scene: An Annotated Bibliography. New Delhi, Abhinav Publications, 1976.

Desai, Ziyauddin
Centres of Islamic Learning in India. Delhi, Publications Division, Ministry of Information and Broadcasting, 1978.

Mosques of India. New Delhi, Publication Division, Ministry of Information and Broadcasting, 1971.

Published Muslim Inscriptions of Rajasthan. Jaipur, Directorate of Archaeology & Museums, 1971.

Dogra, R.C.
Catalogue of the Early Printed Books on South Asia: From 1586 to 1864 held in the Library of School of Oriental and African Studies, London. New Delhi, Aditya Prakashan, 1988.

Jammu and Kashmir: A Select and Annotated Bibliography of Manuscripts, books and articles together with a survey of its history, languages and literature from Rajatarangini to Modern Times. Delhi, Ajanta Pub., 1986.

Durrany, K.S.
Religion in Society: Selected Indian press index of comparative Religion. New Delhi, Uppal Pub. House, 1983.

Eminent Mussalmans. New Delhi, Neeraj Pub. House, 1981 (rpt.)

Encyclopaedia of Indian Literature. New Delhi, Sahitya Akademi, 1977.

Fehervari, G. and Y.H. Safdari.
1400 years of Islamic Art: A Descriptive Catalogue. London, Khalili Gallery, 1981.

Geddes, C.L.
Guide to reference books for Islamic Studies. Denver, American Institute of Islamic Studies, 1985.

George, K.M. ed.
Comparative Indian Literature. Trivandrum, Kerala Sahitya Akademi, 1983.

Ghalib Academy, Ghalib Bibliography, New Delhi, 1970.

Gidwani N.N. and K. Navalani,
Guide to Reference Material on India. Jaipure, Sarawati Pub. 1974. 2 V.

Glasse, Cyril.
Concise encyclopaedia of Islam. London, Stacey International, 1989.

Grimwood, Jones, D.
Arab Islamic Bibliography, Hassocks, Harvester Press, 1977.

Guide to Delhi, Ed.2. New Delhi, Indian Tourism Development Corp. 1982.

Gurney, Gene.
Kingdoms of Asia: The Middle East and Africa; An illustrated encyclopedia of ruling monarchs from ancient times to the present. New York, Crown, 1986.

Habib, Irfan
Atlas of the Mughal Empire: Political and economic maps with detailed notes, bibliography and index. Aligarh, Aligarh Muslim Univ. 1982.

Hai, M.A.
Hanbook of Islam, Delhi, Maktaba Alhasnat, 1984.

Haq, Abdul
Practical advanced twentieth century dictionary: English into English and Urdu. Comp. by Bashir Ahmed Qureshi. New Delhi, Anjum Book Depot., 1989. (Student edition).

Practical Standard twentieth century dictionary: Urdu into English. Comp. by Bashir Ahmed Qureshi. New Delhi, Anjum Book Depot, 1988 (Student edition)

Standard English-Urdu Dictionary, Delhi, J.S. Sant Singh and Sons, 1975.

Haroon, Mohammed
Cataloguing of Indian. Muslim Names. Delhi, Indian Bibliographies Bureau, 1987.

Muslims of India: Their Literature on Education, History, Politics, Religion, Socio-Economic and Communal Problems. New Delhi, Indian Bibliographies Bureau, 1989.

Hasan, Masud-ul
Daughters of Islam: Being short biographical Sketches of 82 famous Muslim Women (including 20 relevant to South Asia.). Lahore; Hazrat Data Ganj Bakhsh Academy, 1976.

Hasan, M.
Historians of Medieval India. Meerut, Meenakshi 1989.

Henderson, J.R.
Coins of Haidar Ali & Tipu Sultan. Delhi, D.K. Publishers Distributors, 1987 (rpt).

Hillmann, Michael. C.
Twentieth century Persian literature in trnaslation: A Bibliography. Washington, Cultural Department, Imperial Embassy of Iran. 1976.

Hingorani, R.P.
Painting in South Asia: A Bibliography. Delhi, Varnasi: Bharatiya Publishing House, 1976.

Husain, Ashraf
Record of all the Puranic and Non-Historical Epigrkaphs on the Protected Monuments in the Delhi Province. New Delhi, Manager of Publications, 198?.

Husain, Mirza Shafique
Kashmir: An Annotated Bibliography. Islamabad, National Institute of Historical & Cultural Research, 1981.

India, National Archives.
Descriptive list of Mutiny papers in the National Archives of India, Bhopal. V.III, Delhi, Manager of Pub., 1970.

India Who's Who, 1988-89. 19th ed. New Delhi, INFA, 1989.

Indian Books in Print. 1988. New Delhi, Indian Bibliographies Bureau, 1988.

Indian Council for Cultural Relations, New Delhi.
Indian Literature: Select Bibliographies. ed. H.S. Patil and Saiyyad Masih Ul-Hasan. New Delhi, Vikas, 1972. (Aspects of Indian Culture,3).

Indian Council of Social Science Research, Southern

Regional Centre, Hyderabad
Select Bibliography of Indian Muslims. Hyderabad, 1983.

Indian Records: Commercial View of the Relations between the British Government and the Nawab Nazims of Bengal, Bihar and Orissa. New Delhi, D.K. Publishers Distribution, 1985 (rpt).

Inter-University Board of India
Bibliography of doctoral dissertations accepted by Indian Universities, 1857-1970. New Delhi, 1975. 5V.

Islahi M, Yusuf
Everyday Fiqh. Tr. Abdul Aziz Kamal. New Delhi, Adam. 1986.

Islamic Heritage of India. New Delhi, National Museum, 1986.

Jafar, Saiyid Mohammad Comp.
Research facilities in Uttar Pradesh. Gurgaon, Haryana, Indian Documentation Service, 1971.

Jain, M.K.
Indian a: A Bibliography of Bibliographical Sources. New Delhi, Concept, 1989.

Jain, N.K.
Biographical Dictionary of Muslims in the Indian sub-continent, 1957-1976. Columbia, South Asia Books, 1978.

Muslims in India: A Biographical Dictionary. New Delhi, Manohar Publications, 1983.

Muslims in India: A Biographical Dictionary. New Delhi, Manohar Publications, 1980.

Jones, Sir William
Grammar of the Persian Language. Delhi, (Distr.: D.K Publishers), 1982.

Joshi, A.K.
"Furthers Reading," (On Indian Muslims) Seminar, No. 174 (Fe. 74), 43-45.

Jotwani, Motilal
Sufis of Sindh. New Delhi, Publications Division, Ministry of I and B., 1986.

Kabir, Kausar and Inamul Kabir
Biographical Dictionary of Prominent Muslim Ladies. New Delhi, Light & Life Publishers, 1983.

Kalia, D.R. and M.K. Jain
Bibliographies of India. New Delhi, Concept, 1974.

Eminent Indians: A Bibliography of Bibliographies. New Delhi, Marwah Publications, 1977.

Kaul, H.K.
Urdu Manuscripts: A Discriptive Bibliography of Manuscripts in Delhi Libraries. New Delhi, Heritage, 1977.

Kesavan, B.S. ed.
National Bibliography of Indian Literature, 1901-1953. Vol. IV: Sindhi, Tamil, Telugu, Urdu. New Delhi, Sahitya Akademi, 1974.

Khalidi, Omar
Dakan (Deccan) under the Sultans, 1296-1724: A bibliography of monographic and periodical literature. Whichita, K.S.: Hayderabad Historical Society, 1987.

Hyderabad State under the Nizams, 1724-1948: A Bibliography of monographic and periodical literature. Wichita. Hayderabad Historical Society, 1986.

Khan, A. Mohammad
Medieval Gujaraj: Its Political and Statistical History Based on Mirat-i-Ahmadi. Tr. James Bird. Delhi, Indian Bibliographies Bureau, 1985.

Khan, A. Saeed, Comp.
Bibliography of the works of Abul Raihan al Biruni. New Delhi, I.N.S.A., 1982.

Khan, I. Alam
Political Biography of a Mughal Noble Munim Khan, Khan-i-Khanan. New Delhi, Oriental Pubs., 1973.

Khan, M.A. Shaheed
Directory of Islamic Libraries and Librarians. California, Islamic Library Association., 1983.

Khan M.A. Wali
Copper Coins of Adil Shahi Dynasty of Bijapur. Hyderabad, Biral Archaeological and Cull. Research Inst., 1980.

Khan, Shafaat A.
Sources for the study of British India in the 17th Century. Delhi: Pankaj Publications, 1986.

Khan, Shaukat Ali
Catalogue of the Arabic Manuscripts: Prayers, dialectics, at Fiqh & Law of Inheritance. V.2. Tonk, Arabic & Persian Research Institute, 1983.

Catalogue of the Arabic Manuscripts: Quranic Sciences and Science of Traditions. Tonk, Arabic & Persian Research Inst, 1980.

Descriptive Catalogue of the Persian Manuscripts. Tonk, Arabic and Persian Research Institute, 1986.

Historical heritage: A bibligraphical survey of the rare manuscripts in the Arabic & Persian Research Institute Rajasthan, Tonk. Arabic & Persian Res. Inst, 1980.

History and Historians of Rajasthan, Delhi, Triveni, 1981.

Kheirie, Alhaj Khan Bahadur, A.A.
Index-cum-concordance for the Holy Quran. New Delhi, Kitab Bhavan, 1988.

Khuda Bakhsh Oriental Public Library
Catalogue of Arabic & Persian Manuscripts in Khuda Bakhsh Library, Patna, V.3. (Persian Poetry) Patna 1977.

Catalogue of Arabic & Persian Manuscripts in Khuda Bakhsh Library, Patna, V.7 (Indian History: Persian), Patna 1977.

Catalogue of Arabic & Persian Manuscripts in Khuda Bakhsh Library, Patna, V 29. (Quranic Science, Arabic). Patna, 1971.

Catalogue of Arabic & Persian Mansucripts in Khuda Baksh Library, Patna V.20 (Tradition: Arabic), Patna, 1970.

Catalogue of Arabic & Persian Manuscripts in Khuda Bakhsh Library, Patna, V.31 (Poetry, along with history, biography, tales & anthology: Persian), Patna, 1977.

Catalogue of Arabic A & Persian Manuscripts in Khuda Bakhsh Library, Patna, V.32 (Encyclopedia, Natural Science, Medicine, Logic & Ethics: Persian), Patna, 1980.

Catalogue of Arabic & Persian Manuscripts in Khuda Bakhsh Library, Patna. V 34. (Jurisprudence: Arabic), Patna, 1980.

Kritzeck, James ed
Anthology of Islamic Literature: From Rise of Islam to Modern Times. New York, New Am. Lib. 1975.

Kumar, Devendra.
"Further Reading" (on Islam) Seminar, No. 290 (Oct. 1983), 46-48.

Kumedan, B.S.
Modernisation and Social Reforms Among the Mulsims-A Select Bibliography. Delhi, Delhi School of Social Work, 1978.

Latif, Sayed Abdul, ed.
Tarjuman-al-Quran. Hyderabad, Syed Abdul Latif Trust for Quranic Cultural Research, 1980.

Lytle, Elizabeth.

Women in India: A Comprehensive Bibliography. Monticello, II., Vance Bibliographies, 1978.

Madan, Som Nath
Freedom Movement in India: A Select Bibliography. Delhi, Anmol Publications, 1987.

Malik, Imam
Muwatta, Tr. M. Rahimuddin, New Delhi, Kitab Bhawan, 1981.

Al-Marghinani, Ali Ibn Bakr
Hedaya or Guide: A Commentary on the Musalman Laws, by Charles Hamilton. 2V, New Delhi, Kitab Bhawan, 1986.

Marshall, D.N
Mughals in India: A Bibliographical survey of manuscripts, London, Mansell, 1985.

Motamar al-Alam al Islami.
Country by country outline survey of Muslim minorities of the world. Karachi, 1977.

Muhammad, Shan, Ed.
Aligarh Movement: Basic document, 1864-1895. 3V. Meerut, Meenakhi, 1978.

Indian Muslims: A Documentary record, 1900-1947. 9V. Meerut, Meenakshi, 1980.

Mukherjee, A.K.
Guide to selected reference tools and Indological source materials, classified and annotated. Calcutta, World Press, 1979.

Musleh, Abu Mohammed
Last Part of Holy Quran (Para Aam). New Delhi, Kitab Bhawan, 1979.

Muslim, Imam
Sahih Muslim. Tr. M. Abdul Hamid Siddiqui 4V, Delhi, Kitab Bhawan, 1984.

Nath, R.
Jharokha : An illustrated glossary of Indo-Muslim architecture. Jaipur: Historical Research Documentation Programme, 1986.

National register of doctoral dissertations accepted and in progress in Social Science and Humanities, in India Universities. Bhopal, Council of Oriental Research, 1980, 2 pts.

Nayar, M.P.,
"Further Reading", (On the Muslim condition), Seminar No.240 (Aug '79), 45-48.

Nazir, Afdal Ahmed.
Haj Guide (Brief Description of Haj performance with English translation of Prayers. Calcutta, Darul Eshaat Islamia, 1970.

Nizami, Khaliq Ahmed:
Maulana Azad Album (Urdu with English translation). New Delhi, D.K. Publishers Distributors, 1988.

Sir Syed album, Delhi, Idarah-i-Adabiyat-i-Delhi, 1984.

Sayyid Ahmed Khan: Bibliography. Delhi, Publications Division, 1974.

Ojha, V.S. Gaurishankar
Corpus inscription Bhavanagar: Being a selection of Arabic & Persian inscription collected by Antiquarian Department, Bhavanagar State, New Delhi, Kumar Bros. 1971.

Pandey, G.
"Liberalism and the study of Indian history: A review of writings on communalism", Eco & Pol. Weekly, 18 (1983), 1789-1794

Pearson, O.D.
South Asian bibliography: A handbook and guide. Hassocks, Sussex, Harvester Press, 1979.

Pickthall M.M.
Holy Quran: Translation with Arabic Text. New Delhi, Kitab Bhawan, 1982.

Pirzada, Shams
Dawatul Quran, Arabic Text, translation and commentary, Tr. A.K. Shaikh Bombay, Idara Dawatul Quran, 1983.

Poonawala, Ismail K.
Bibliography of Ismaili Literature. Malibu, Undena Pub., 1977.

Pritchett, Francis, W.
Urdu literature: A bibliography of English source. New Delhi, Manohar, 1979.

Qadir, Abdul
Famous Urdu poets and writers. New Delhi, Seemant Prakashan, 1977.

Rahman, Afzal-ur
Subject index of the Holy Quran. New Delhi, Noor Publishing House, 1987.

Rajannan, Busnagi
South Indian Studies: abstracts of American doctoral dissertations relating to South India. Salem, Institute of Kongu Studies, 1981.

Ram, Sadhu
Index to 'Indian Historical Quarterly,' 1929-1963. Delhi, Munshiram Manohar lal, 1970.

Ramaswami, N.S.
Mamallapuram: An Annotated bibliography. Madras: New Era Publishers, 1980.

Razi, F.D.
Modern Persian dictionary (Persian-Urdu-English). New Delhi, Kitab Bhawan, 1981.

Richards, J.F. ed.
Document forms for official orders of appointment in the Mughal Empire. Cambridge, Gibb Memorial Trust, 1986.

Rodgers, C.J.
Catalogue of the coins: The coins of the Mughal Emperors of India in 4 Vols. New Delhi, D.K. Publishers & Distributors, 1985. (rpt).

Rothermund, D.
Islam in South Asia: A survey of current research, London, Steiner, Franz. 1975.

S.N.D.T. University. Research Unit on Women Studies.
Select Bibliography on Women in India. Bombay, Allied Publishers, 1975.

Sabri, M. and A.B. Ghairat
English-Urdu-Pushto-Persian conversation. Lahore, Maliks Book Depot, 1986.

Saiyed, A.R.
"Islam & Muslims in recent social science literature - a Review of selected articles", in Islam in India. Studies and Commentaries. ed. C.W. Troll V.1. New Delhi, Vikas, 1982.

Sakala, Carol.
Women of South Asia: A Guide to resources. Millwood, N.Y., Kraus International, 1980.

Salar Jung Museum
Journeys in Art Through the Salar Jung Museum. Hyderabad, Salar Jung Museum Board, 1971.

Sastri, P.P. Subrahmanya
Descriptive catalogue of the Islamic manuscripts in the Govt. Oriental Manuscripts Library, Madras, 5V. Govt. of Madras, 197.

Satyaprakash,
Muslims in India: A Bibliography of Their Religious, Socio-Economic and Political Literature. Gurgaon, Indian Documentation Service, 1984.

Sexena, Ram Babu.
European and Indo-European Poets of Urdu and Persian. Jaipur, Historical Research Documentation Programme (Distributor), 1977 (Rpt).

Schimmel, Annemarie
Islamic Literatures of India (History of Indian Literature Series. V.7. Fasc.1. Part 1) Wiesbaden, Otto Harrasowitz, 1973.

Select Bibliography (on Islam), Cultural News from India, 17:3 (July 1976), 112-119.

Selections from the Journal of the Punjab Historical Society. 3 Vols. Jaipur, Historical Research Documentation Programme, (Distributor), 1982.

Sengupta, Benoyendra
Indian reference and information sources: An annotated bibliography of select reference and representative books and periodicals, on different aspects of Indian Life and Culture. Calcutta, World Press, 1981.

Seton, Rosemary,
Indian 'Mutiny' 1857-1856: A Guide to source material in the Indian officer Library and Records. London: The British Library, 1986.

Shackle, C.
"Some Categories for the comparative study of the medieval Muslims Literature of the Indus region", Punjab Univ. J. Medieval Indian Lit. 1:1 (Sept. 77), 3-13.

Shakir, Moin.
Muslim Attitude: A trend report and bibliography. Aurangabad, Parimal Prakashan, 1974.

Sharma, D.C.
"Further Reading: Muslims", Seminar, No.125 (Jan. 70), 44-47.

Sharma, H.D.

Indian Reference Sources: An annotated guide to Indian reference material, Varanasi, Indian Bibliographic Centre, (V.1) 1988 (V.2) 1989.

Sharma, Jagdish Saran
Sources of Indian Civilization: A Bibliography of works by world orientalists other than Indian. Delhi, Vikas, 1974.

Sharma, Jagdish, N.
India's Minorities: A Bibliographical Study. New Delhi, Vikas, 1975.

Sharma, Sri Ram
Bibliography of Moghul India, A.D. 1526-1767. Bombay, Karnataka Publishing House, 1970.

Siddiqi, Iqtidar Husain
"Modern Writings of Islam and Muslims in India", Studies in Islam 8: 1-14, (Jan-Oct. 1971).

Siddiqi, M. Suleman and M. Ahmadullah
Index of Islamic Culture: Subject Author and Reviews, 1927-1980. Hyderabad, Islamic Culture Board, 1984.

Singh, Mohindar, Comp.
Learned societies and institutions in India, activities and publications. Including over 4,000 research oriented titles. Delhi, Metropolitan Books, 1975.

Sinha, K. and Q. Lutfi
Bibliography on Communal (Hindu Muslim) Tensions (Pilot fasciules). New Delhi, Documentation Centre, Gandhi Peace Foundation, 1970.

Bibliography on Kashmir Problems. New Delhi, Documentation Centre, Gandhi Peace Foundation, 1970.

Smart, E. and D.S. Walker
Pride of the Princes: Indian Art of the Mughal Era in the Cincinnati Art Museum Cincinnati, Ohio: Cincinnati Art Museum, 1986.

Steingass, F.
Learner's Arabic-English Dictionary, New Delhi, Sterling, 1986.

Learner's English Arabic Dictionary, New Delhi, Sterling, 1986.

Taher, Mohammed and Abdul Majeed Pangal
Bibliographical Control of Islamic Literature in India; Perspectives', Islamic Culture, 58:2 (April 1984), 161-169.

Titley, Norah M.
Miniatures from Persian manuscripts. A catalogue and subject index of paintings from Persia, Indian and Turkey in the British Library and the British Museum. London British Museum Publications Ltd. for British Library, 1977.

Tyagi, K.G.
Foreign researchers on Indian political systems & processes. Delhi, Pinka Agencies, 1984.

Usmani, Muh. Adil and Nasim Fatima
Books on Allama Iqbal in university libraries of Pakistan: Allama Iqbal birth centenary celebrations. 1977. Karachi: University, 1977. (Karachi University Library Publications).

Vashishta, B.K. ed.
Encyclopaedia of Indian women, 1976. New Delhi, Praveen Encyclopaedia Publications, 1976.

Viquar S. Nasiruddin.
5000 years Gregorian Calendar with comparative table of Hegiri & Gregarian dates. Hyderabad Imam-Ul Uloom Education Society, 1983.

Wagle, Iqbal
Reference aids to South Asia. Toronto: University of Toronto Library, 1977. (Its reference series No.22).

Who's Who of Indian Women, International. Madras, National Biographical Centre, 1977.

Who's who of Indian Writers, 1983. New Delhi, Sahitya Akademy, 1983.

Yaqin, Anwarul and Badar Anwar
Protection of women under the law: An annotated bibliography. New Delhi, Deep & Deep, 1982.

Young, K.K. and Arvind Sharma.
Images of feminine-mythic, philosophic and human - in the Buddhist, Hindu and Islamic traditions: A bibliography of women in India. Chico, Calif.: New Horizons Press, 1974.

Zbavitel, Dusan ed.
Dictionary of Oriental Literatures, V.2; South and South-east Asia. New York: Basic Books, 1974.

AUTHOR INDEX

KEYWORD SUBJECT INDEX

TITLE INDEX